# SKI-RUNNING

# SKI-RUNNING

## KATHARINE FURSE

**WILDSIDE PRESS**

**SKI-RUNNING**

Published by Wildside Press LLC.
www.wildsidebooks.com

# PREFACE

So many excellent books have been written about skiing that it is, perhaps, presumptuous on my part to think that there is room for another.

Mr. Vivien Caulfeild in his "How to Ski" and "Skiing Turns," as well as Mr. Arnold Lunn in his "Skiing for Beginners," "Cross Country Skiing" and "Alpine Skiing," have covered all the ground of the technique discovered up to date. What future discoveries and inventions may be made, requiring new books, no one knows as yet.

Had it not been for the help and coaching these two exponents of skiing have given to me personally, I should never have been able to enjoy the sport to the extent I do now, because I should probably have been content to continue running across country, falling whenever I wanted to stop, and using a kick turn at the end of my traverses. Their enthusiasm and example gave me new ideas of the standard I wanted to attain, and their unfailing kindness and advice helped me to get nearer to it than I could otherwise have done.

The standard still lies away up out of reach, as age undoubtedly tells against the Ski-runner, and the perfect Christiania in deep, soft snow round trees growing close together on a steep slope must be done in heaven rather than on earth by people who are nearer fifty than forty.

Much experience of coaching beginners convinces me that there is still room for a book such as I hope to make this—a book containing only the simple answers to questions put to me during the last three years, when I have been responsible for running the skiing in various centres. The object of such coaching is to raise the standard of British skiing, and it is satisfactory to realize that other nations, including the Swiss, already marvel at the fair average of our runners. This is specially remarkable when it is remembered that most British runners can only afford a bare fortnight or three weeks' winter holiday in the Alps, and that they are not always in training when they arrive. Skiing is a sport which exercises every nerve and muscle as well as lungs, as is soon discovered during the first 100 feet climb or the first fall in deep snow on the Nursery slopes.

In addition to my conviction that there is room for another book for beginners, my love of the Alps, which have been my home for the greater part of my life, also induces me to try to show something of the real objects of skiing; namely getting to the silent places which can only be reached on skis, realizing something of the strength and immensity of Nature at her grimmest, profiting by the wonderful atmosphere of the mountains, to say nothing of the beauty of an Alpine view on a fine day.

The greatest pity is that most British winter holiday-makers can only go out for Christmas. This is admittedly the worst time from the point of view of weather. At low altitudes rain often falls early in January, turning the snow into slush and reducing the Ski-er to despair. After the 15th January, the weather is usually better, and in February the days are longer and finer. The best time of all for an Alpine holiday is usually February and early March. My advice to novices, who are not tied by Christmas holidays, is to come out about the 20th January, when the hotels are less crowded, the days longer, the snow more certain and all the conditions more favourable. Some of my own best skiing days have been late in March when the crocuses and gentians were already opening to the sun on the Southern slopes, and a soldanella might be found along some tiny stream. Few experiences can equal a Spring day among the Alps when the wealth of flowers begins to show in the valleys, while masses of good snow still lie on the Northern slopes or on the ridges above 6,000 feet.

Early starts are necessary these days as the sun blazes after 11 a.m., but nothing can equal the bodily comfort and well-being enjoyed at mid-day, lunching at the top of some peak or pass, basking in the blaze and imagining the run down cool slopes. No Ski-runner, who has not been out in late February or March, realizes the joy and comfort of late skiing. The hotels will remain open as long as clients stay to make it worth while, and all the mid-winter amenities will be kept up if they are wanted.

In recommending places and equipment, I intend boldly to confine myself to the places I have been to and to the equipment I have used, or of which I have had reports from people I trust. This is a somewhat risky determination as there is great competition among the various centres and business firms which cater for Ski-runners. My reason is that the endless advertisements must be extremely confusing to the novice, who does not know what to believe, and who may sometimes be let down by a glowing description of some place or gear, which proves to be quite unsuitable.

The old hands will find nothing new in this book. Not even contro-versy about the nomenclature of turns or as to which foot should carry the weight in a Christiania. My own view of skiing turns is that they are a means to an end, and not an end in themselves, and that the Ski-runner, who is content to spend weeks on the Nursery slopes, perfecting one turn, has wasted almost weeks, when he might be enjoying what Skis enable one to reach among the mountains above. At the same time every beginner should be content to devote two or three of his first days to the Nursery slopes, learning the elements of good skiing before dashing off on an excursion. As I know from painful experience, there is much to unlearn in what one has picked up by the light of Nature. Scrambling down a run, crashing and sitting on one's Skis, may be great fun the first day, but is tiring and humiliating as time goes on. It is infinitely preferable to learn the knack of skiing tidily, and thereby keeping dry and, in a few days, running well enough thoroughly to enjoy a day out with its slow climb to the top of some peak or pass, and then the slide down under control.

This is where tests are so valuable. Most people undoubtedly enjoy competition and, if the passing of the turns is made a necessary qualification for the timed run of the 3rd class test, most beginners will determine to learn them and then to try the Run and, having successfully passed that, wear a Badge. Badge-hunting, like pot-hunting, may not be a very worthy object in itself, but if it encourages people to become proficient in a beautiful sport, let us give our weakness of character free play and achieve the results it leads to. The tests of the Federated Ski Clubs of Great Britain have done more to raise the standard of our running than anything else imaginable.

The beginner is wise, who chooses a centre where the skiing is well organized, and where he can be certain of getting coaching as well as excursions suited to his standard, as nothing is lonelier than going to a place where he is dependent on his own initiative; neither is anything more irksome to the good runner than to be asked to admit a stranger to his party, who may keep him back and spoil his run. This will be further alluded to in the Chapter on Etiquette, and if a beginner wishes to be popular, I advise him strongly to adhere to the "Law." A strict code has been adopted, mainly as a result of the suffering from pertinacious runners, who put their standard higher than is admitted by others.

Where the skiing is organized, tests sort different individuals into their different standards and Runs are planned accordingly, so that the novice is not over-strained and the experienced runner is not hindered by too big a party.

The beginner should also choose a centre where there is a railway to help him. A great deal of precious time and energy may be wasted in a short holiday when all climbing has to be done on skis. The first runs are tiring enough without the additional fatigue of climbing, and going up in a funicular or railway opens up numbers of runs which would be far too energetic for most people who are not in training.

# HISTORY OF SKIING

Very little is known of the early history of skiing. Doctor Henry Hoek in his book "Der Schi" gives a very interesting chapter tracing the use of Skis back to the earliest records. He thinks that Skis were used by Central Asian races thousands of years B.C. and long before they were used in Europe. According to his book the word "Schi" is derived from the Gothic "Skaidan," the German "Scheiden," Latin "Scindere," and so on. All these words mean split or divide, and might be used to describe the split wood of which Skis are made or their action in dividing or separating the snow through which they pass.

Doctor Hoek further says that early records show how skiing was a sport practised by knights, and he quotes Rognwald of Orkney (1159 A.D.) who states that he could run on Skis.

The Swedish Bishop Magnus writes in 1533 of the way in which the Norwegians used Skis for traversing country when hunting.

During the Swedish and Norwegian war in 1808 the Norwegian Army included 2,000 Ski runners, but the use of Skis does not seem to have come into warfare again until the Great War of 1914-1918, when the Swiss, Austrians and Italians all used them on the Alpine frontiers.

The modern and fully recorded use of Skis began about 1843 when the sport became really popular in Norway and a Ski race was run at Tromso. In 1861 a Ski Club was founded, and in 1863 an exhibition was held there.

The Swedes also took up skiing as a sport at about this time but Skis do not seem to have penetrated into Central Europe until after 1870 when a French doctor tried them at Chamounix in 1871.

The first introduction of Skis into Switzerland, which I have been able to trace, was by the monks of St. Bernard, who obtained some pairs from Norway in 1883, thinking that they might be useful in their work of mercy, rescuing pedestrians who were in difficulties on the Pass. About 1887 Colonel Napier came to Davos bringing with him a Norwegian man-servant and a pair of Skis. Mythical tales were told of the way this man slid down the slopes from châlet to hotel, carrying a tea tray on his shoulder. I have only a vague recollection of seeing him perform, but when Colonel Napier left Davos the same year, he gave the Skis to me to play with. They were very similar to modern Skis but had a rigid binding made of sealskin with no means of tightening or loosening it. Not knowing better, I used to try to run in gouties or rubber snow-boots which slipped about inside the binding so that I had absolutely no control. This did not make much difference, as I knew nothing of the art and only used the Skis as a freak on days off from tobogganing. I knew nothing of wax, and when the Skis stuck, they stuck, and I thought it a poor game. When they slid I sat down and I thought it a poorer game. It never entered my head that I could traverse across any slope and so I always went straight down and only by a fluke did I ever stand. Then Tobias Branger, who was a great sportsman and kept a sports shop at Davos, imported several pairs of Skis and practised the art himself.

About this time Sir Arthur Conan Doyle and Mr. and Mrs. Hugh Dobson took up the game and we spent many hours practising on the slopes behind Davos Dorf.

The Richardson brothers, who had been to Norway, came to Davos about 1893 bringing with them knowledge of the sport and soon gathered round them a keen lot of disciples. The Davos English Ski Club was formed and from now on skiing spread rapidly throughout Switzerland.

In the meantime, Ski Clubs were also being formed in the Black Forest and other parts of Germany, as well as in Austria.

Doctor Nansen, in his book about Greenland, described the use of Skis for Arctic exploration and his accounts fired a great many more people to try the game.

I advise anyone who wishes to know more of the development of Ski running to read Doctor Hoek's book "Der Schi," published in 1922, as he gives a long account of the first forming of Clubs as well as the gradual adoption of Skis as a means to winter climbing, and, further, a useful list of the literature on the subject.

After the first beginnings in 1899, the Swiss became energetic and enthusiastic runners. The children could be seen on barrel staves with a pair of old boots nailed to the centre into which they slipped their feet with their own boots on. It was not a particularly graceful game in those days. Runners armed themselves with poles some 8 feet long on which they leant heavily when running downhill. This school soon gave way to the more modern school, which proved that the carrying of two sticks was better than one only. A great many books on the technique of skiing followed each other fast and furiously—Zdarsky and Lilienfeld, Caulfeild and Lunn, Roget Hoeg and others all contributing to the controversy on technique.

Now there are innumerable Ski Clubs with their own year-books, and the sport is so well launched, not only in Europe, but also in Australia, New Zealand, East Africa and America and elsewhere, throughout the world, that there is but little chance of its ever again dying out.

The British Ski Clubs include the Ski Club of Great Britain, the British Ski Association, the Alpine Ski Club and the Ladies' Ski Club. These are federated in one Council and work harmoniously together for the furtherance of British skiing.

This is a very incomplete history, but I feel that it is better to limit it to a few dates and to await the publishing of a more extensive history of skiing in English than now exists.

# COST OF A SKIING HOLIDAY IN WINTER

The expenses of a winter holiday differ according to the place chosen, the hotel and the organization to whose care you commit yourself, if any. Any figures I quote are approximate and are subject to change owing to fluctuations in exchanges, etc.

If you go to a large hotel, with all its luxuries, you will pay anything from £1 a day upwards, and this may not include sports tax, etc. The smaller hotels will probably make arrangements for pension at about 16 francs, or even 14 francs, or less, per day, but may not be very comfortable, and comfort is important in winter. It is particularly necessary that the hotel should be well heated, as the drying of skiing clothes is a very important point.

As I said in my Preface, the beginner will be wise who chooses a centre where the sports are highly organized, and where he will be certain to find coaching and arrangements made for tests and runs, as well as a railway or funicular to help with uphill work. Only in such a place can he learn enough skiing in a short time to enable him to begin to enjoy touring before he returns home, panting to come out again and continue the experience. One joy of skiing is that you usually begin again where you left off, and have not to relearn what you learnt the winter before.

Having lived in the Alps off and on for forty-six years, and having seen all sorts of different ways of running things, I realized at Mürren, where I first learnt to ski properly four years ago, how much the beginner profits by going to such a centre. Otherwise he may waste infinite time in skiing without skill and with only half the enjoyment. It is not only at Mürren that the coaching is given, though Mr. Arnold Lunn's system of helping everyone originated there. Pontresina provides it also, and Klosters and other places as well, but it seems to me that Mürren is the mother of up-to-date British skiing.

The cost of a fortnight at a good hotel comes to about £15, including sports tax, afternoon tea and heating. The journey about £7 return 2nd-class or £9 1st-class, in addition. This can be reduced by travelling 3rd class in England and Switzerland, where at any rate it is quite possible to travel 3rd class on any mountain railway.

In addition to the expense of Pension at an hotel and of the journey, at least £5 will probably be required for local railway fares, subscription to entertainment fund, baths, gratuities, hire of Skis, lessons, guides, etc. £30 ought to cover a fortnight, and £35 three weeks, and a good deal less can be reckoned if a smaller hotel be chosen.

Most of the Sports Hotels will now quote an inclusive price per day, to which at least 10 per cent. should be added to the estimate for gratuities to servants. This is the recognized scale at which gratuities are given by most people, though they might often amount to more when any special service has been rendered.

Local railway fares on mountain railways are high, because of the great expense of keeping them open, but most of these railways offer special sports tickets, either for a definite period as a season ticket, or for a certain number of journeys. For instance, on the Muottas Muraigl Funicular Railway above Pontresina 24 tickets single journey can be obtained for the sum of Frs. 50, while the ordinary single fare is Frs. 4.75, or more than twice the reduced fare.

The cost of equipment must be added to the estimate, but this need not be very great as skiing boots and gloves are the only items which cannot usually be used at home by men—trousers or breeches being an additional cost for women.

People sometimes complain that a Swiss winter holiday is very costly, but I believe it can compare favourably with a golfing holiday at home. Skiing is the cheapest possible sport, if runners are content to foot it uphill instead of using railways or sledges. During the months of February and March, special low terms can probably be obtained in the hotels, as they are anxious to prolong their season, and will do anything they can afford to induce British sportsmen to come out then. February and the first half of March are the best time from every point of view, so that no one who can take his holiday then, and who does not want all the gaiety of the social side, will regret going during these months. In old days before the war this was fully appreciated and the season used to last three months, instead of a short six weeks as it does now.

# SKIING CENTRES

In this chapter I propose only to describe such of the larger Swiss places as I know personally, or by reputation. There are a great many smaller places where equally good, or even better, Skiing may be found, but, as my book is meant mainly for beginners, it seems preferable to adhere to the advice given in the preface, and for me to mention only such centres as provide comfort in the hotels and good coaching and organization of tours, as well as facilities for playing other games. Most people when they go to the Alps for their first winter visit wish to try all the different sports in order to see which they like best, and there seems to me to be no question but that the all-round sportsman gets the most out of his holiday.

There may be days when skiing is not possible or when a few hours on the rink or toboggan run offer a relief to a stale Ski runner. It is usually only the really keen enthusiast of some years' standing who can spend the whole day waxing or oiling his Skis, or poring over a map planning future runs.

When choosing a place the first objective is a good supply of snow. This does not seem to depend entirely on height, though there is more likelihood of finding it above 4,000 feet than below that height. Above 5,000 feet there is less chance of thaw and rain—the bugbears of all Winter sportsmen, who can only go out for the Christmas holidays.

I have known a Winter when snow has lain in one district at 5,000 feet and not at 6,000 feet in another, but this was exceptional. The higher you go, the more hope you have of snow as a rule and also of frost, which is so necessary to keep the snow in good condition.

The centres I recommend are mainly arranged in groups geographically, taking the Canton of Graubunden, or the Grisons first, because it is the country I love best, having spent most of my early life there. The heights are taken from Murray's Handbook.

**KLOSTERS**, 3,970 feet above the sea. This seems to me to be one of the very best Winter Sports centres. It is a small village with two large and a few small hotels. It usually has good snow and is protected from wind. There is plenty of sun, but North slopes provide good runs near the village as well as on the Parsenn.

The Rhaetische Railway helps runners to get the maximum of downhill running for the minimum of climb, especially opening up the whole Parsenn district to those who want a long day's tour with only some 1-1/2 hours' climb.

The Nursery slopes are good, and there is plenty of open ground near the hotels for practice. The skiing is well organized by the local club, and there are 1st-class Ski Instructors, as well as Certificated Guides.

The rinks are well kept and the Klosters run of old renown is maintained in good condition for tobogganing or bobbing.

There is quite a good Ski map to be obtained locally, but the Ordnance Map should be used as well.

Skis can be hired locally.

**DAVOS**, 5,015 feet above the sea, was one of the first places at which Winter sports began, and it still offers almost everything desired by the Ski runner. The fact that Davos is much visited by invalids deters a great many people from going there, for fear of infection. As a matter of fact they are probably a good deal safer there than in some other places where there may be a few invalids, but where the same precautions regarding disinfection may not be taken.

Two or three hotels are kept open for sports people only, and at these the life is just the same as in all the other well-known centres.

Davos is within very easy reach by the Rhaetische Railway of all the Parsenn runs. The side valleys, Fluela, Dischma and Sertig, all offer innumerable good runs to the energetic runner who does not object to climbing, and there are endless Nursery slopes. It is one of the few places whence tours can still be planned over almost unlimited snowfields when a track is a rare sight except on the few ordinary short runs or on the Parsenn.

The local club organizes the skiing, and good Ski Instructors and Guides are available.

The rinks are excellent and the Schatzalp and Klosters runs are maintained for bobbing and tobogganing.

There is a good Ski map showing all the runs round Davos, but the Ordnance Map should be used as well.

Skis can be hired locally.

**AROSA**, 5,643 feet above the sea, is said to be excellent for skiing, but I do not know it well. There is no railway to help runners much. Invalids go there as well as to Davos, but the same precautions are taken as at Davos.

There are rinks and a very good run for bobbing and tobogganing.

**LENZERHEIDE**, about 4,500 feet above the sea, has a fine reputation for easy skiing. There is no railway to help it and all uphill work has to be done on Skis. I have never been there in Winter-time, but know that a great many runners speak well of Lenzerheide. The skiing is organized, and good Instructors and Guides are available.

There is probably a good rink, but of this I have no personal knowledge.

In the Engadine[1] valley, which is also part of Graubunden, the following centres can be recommended.

**PONTRESINA**, 5,916 feet above the sea. The Nursery slopes are very extensive and offer short runs to the beginner. The Muottas Muraigl funicular conveys runners up some 2,000 feet, when after an easy climb of one hour a really good run may be obtained back to Pontresina.

The Rhaetische and Bernina Railways open up a large number of good runs in the Engadine valley and also up the Bernina and Morteratsch districts.

Open wood-running as well as glacier-running under safe conditions can be enjoyed near home, and Pontresina is undoubtedly one of the best places for people who want to perfect their cross-country running under different conditions.

There are no short afternoon runs ending in the village, but the railways enable people to enjoy all the tours of the Upper Engadine.

The longer tours, such as those over the Kesch Glacier to Bergün or Davos, are unequalled so far as I know.

Having spent two Winters at Pontresina, I can recommend it from intimate knowledge, but only for the real beginner or for the expert who wants amusing running. It is not the place for Ski-ers who only want a short run between lunch and tea.

First-class Guides and good Instructors are available. The skiing is organized and plenty of coaching is given to members of the Public Schools Alpine Sports Club.

Excellent rinks and short bobbing and tobogganing runs are maintained.

A useful guide describing all the runs in the Upper Engadine can be obtained locally.

Skis can be hired locally.

**ST. MORITZ**, 6,037 feet above the sea.
**CELERINA**, 5,750 feet above the sea.
**SAMADEN**, 5,669 feet above the sea.

All three are all served by the Rhaetische and Bernina Railway, and have the same skiing facilities as Pontresina.

---

1    There is apt to be a certain amount of wind in the whole Engadine but its height counterbalances this by usually ensuring that there is not a thaw, even at Christmas time.

Their rinks and toboggan runs are well maintained, those at St. Moritz being, of course, among the best in Switzerland.

Good Guides and Ski Instructors are available, but, so far as I know, skiing is not in any way organized for beginners in these places.

Skis can be hired locally.

**ZUOZ**, 5,617 feet above the sea, is also a good skiing centre further down the Inn Valley. There are only two or three hotels, and the village is quite unspoilt. It provides the most wonderful open South slopes for skiing and North slopes are also within reach across the valley.

Zuoz lies almost at the foot of the climb for the Kesch runs and also taps the country further down the Inn valley behind Schuls.

So far as I know the skiing is not organized in any way, but Guides are available.

There are rinks, but, Zuoz being still one of the old-fashioned places, life would be quiet there.

**CAMPFER**, about 5,850 feet above the sea, and

**SILS-MARIA** and **SILVAPLANA**, about 5,950 feet above the sea, lie further up the Inn valley beyond St. Moritz. No railway exists to help Ski runners, and the slopes are somewhat steep and apt to be precipitous except in the Fex Thal, south of Sils-Maria, which has lovely snow-fields.

Campfer and Silvaplana tap the country lying behind the Julier Pass, but, as no railway helps here, the tours entail a lot of climbing and a drive on the way home.

**MALOJA**, 5,935 feet above the sea, lies at the upper end of the Inn valley.

Never having been there in Winter, I cannot describe it during that season.

It is a beautiful place in Summer, and may open up a good deal of country which is not much tracked, as there is no village and only one large and two small hotels.

The post road runs zigzagging down into Italy and is said to provide a very fine bob or toboggan run. A Rink is kept open. Now that Maloja is being opened as a Winter centre, every amenity for a Winter holiday will probably be offered.

The Bernese Oberland is also one of the best skiing districts in Switzerland.

Mr. A. Lunn has produced a very helpful guide to all the skiing tours and also, with the help of Herr Gurtner, a first-class skiing map, using the Ordnance Map as its basis, so that only one map need be carried.

**MÜRREN**, 5,368 feet above the sea, seems to me to be one of the very best centres for beginners as they receive so much help, and there are numbers of short runs aided by the Allmendhubel funicular which runs up some 700 feet above the village. From the top of this several short runs end in the village or on the Berner Oberland Railway, which brings the tired novice home without much effort.

The Berner Oberland and the Wengern Alp Railways also enable people to get the best of the Scheidegg runs down to Wengen or Grindelwald.

The skiing is very highly organized at Mürren and beginners receive a great deal of help and encouragement.

There are Guides and Instructors.

The Rinks and bob run are admittedly among the best in Switzerland.

Skis can be hired locally.

**WENGEN**, 4,187 feet above the sea, is a lovely place, with the most beautiful view of the Jungfrau. It faces south, but provides two or three nice home runs, which remain in good condition except for the tracks of innumerable runners.

The Wengern Alp Railway is usually open to the Scheidegg, though after a very heavy snow-fall it may take a few days to clear. This enables people to enjoy all the runs down to Grindelwald, returning to Wengen by train.

The skiing is organized and there are good Guides and Instructors. Rinks and a most amusing toboggan run provide for off-days.

Skis can be hired locally.

**GRINDELWALD**, 3,468 feet above the sea, is too well-known as a Summer resort to need much description here.

Its main fault in Winter is that the sun disappears behind a mountain for about an hour and a half in the middle of the day. This ensures perfect ice on the rinks and does not much affect the Ski runner, who can climb beyond the shadow for lunch. I cannot resist mentioning my good friend Frau Wolther's tea-shop as one of the great attractions at Grindelwald, drawing many a Ski runner over the Scheidegg from Mürren and Wengen! Frau Wolther's unfailing welcome and hospitality are a great joy at the end of a hot, wet run, and the fact that a change of clothes can be sent round by train to her care is a great comfort to those coming from afar.

There are plenty of short Ski runs above Grindelwald, and the Scheidegg railway is kept open as far as Alpiglen to help with the climb on a long day's tour.

There are good Guides to be had, some of whom are probably Ski Instructors.

The Rinks are first-class and both bob and toboggan runs are kept up. Skis can be hired locally.

**LAUTERBRUNNEN**, about 3,000 feet above the sea. People who know Switzerland well may wonder why I include Lauterbrunnen in my list, but I have often wondered equally why no one makes it a centre for skiing. Though the sun may not shine there for long hours, the fact that it lies at the junction of the Berner Oberland Railway, the Mürren Funicular and the Wengern Alp Railway seems to me to make it a very possible skiing centre.

There are good hotels, and the Herr Gurtners, whose home Lauterbrunnen is, may be depended upon as two of the best Ski runners in Switzerland and two of the most active pushers of skiing, to do their utmost to help any British runners who decide to try Lauterbrunnen.

All the Mürren, Wengen and Grindelwald runs are within easy reach of Lauterbrunnen, and if the railways will sell special tickets, the cost of the journeys should not be prohibitive.

To my mind, the fact that one could stop at Lauterbrunnen after a day over the Scheidegg would be a great comfort, as the last journey up to Mürren or Wengen is apt to be tiresome after a long run, if often repeated.

In any case it seems to me that runners might do worse than write to Herr Gurtner at Lauterbrunnen and ask for particulars, at any rate for the Christmas holidays, when most of the popular villages are very full and the hotel rates are high.

Good Guides are available at Lauterbrunnen.

**KANDERSTEG**, 3,835 feet above the sea. I have never been there except in Summer when I know it well.

One great attraction about Kandersteg is that it can be reached by a through train from Calais or Boulogne.

From the skiing point of view, I think Kandersteg might be disappointing to the runner who hopes for short runs. There are excellent Nursery slopes, and the Loetschberg Railway probably opens up quite a lot of country.

Guides are obtainable.

Rinks and toboggan runs are maintained.

**ADELBODEN**, 4,450 feet above the sea, is said to be an excellent skiing centre, but I do not know it personally, having only just been up there in Summer time.

There is no railway to help, so that all climbing has to be done on Skis. It is within reach of very good tours throughout the lower Bernese mountains.

The British Championship was held there in 1923, which shows that the skiing is organized, and good Guides are, no doubt, obtainable.

Adelboden, being a well-known Winter Sports Centre, the rink and toboggan runs are probably excellent, but, never having seen them, I cannot vouch for them.

Skis can be hired locally.

**SAANENMOSER**, 4,209 feet above the sea, lies at the top of the low pass between the Simmen Valley above Zweizimme and the Sarine Valley running down to Gstaad and Chateau d'Oex.

There is only the one Sports Hotel and no village. It is a most charming place within reach of skiing in all directions among the lower Bernese mountains.

The Montreux Oberland Railway running down both sides of the Pass helps a little by carrying Ski runners home after some long excursions, but all uphill work has to be done on Skis. The slopes are gradual and the Saanenmoser runs are perfect for people who have learnt the elements of skiing in some active place, and who then want to gain confidence by free running over easy country.

The skiing was not organized when I was at Saanenmoser in 1921, and neither Guides nor Ski Instructors were obtainable. There was only a tiny rink and no toboggan or bob runs.

Skis can be hired at Gstaad.

**GSTAAD**, about 3,800 feet above the sea, lies below Saanenmoser, and is a large village with numbers of hotels. The skiing is very much the same as at Saanenmoser and the Railway serves the same purpose, only helping runners a little.

I have never stayed at Gstaad, but have heard it well spoken of as a Winter Sports centre offering all the usual attractions.

Skis can be hired locally, I believe, and Guides are obtainable.

\* \* \* \* \*

The Rhone Valley offers a few centres which I do not know in Winter. Among those I have heard most about, the following are outstanding.

**VILLARS**, 4,000 feet above the sea, is reached by a railway from Bex. It lies on slopes facing South, and I gather that the skiing there is somewhat limited.

The rinks are said to be good and the usual Winter attractions are offered.

**MONTANA**, 5,000 feet above the sea, is reached by a funicular railway from Sierre. Like Villars it also lies on slopes, facing almost south, but there seems to be good skiing among the mountains behind.

**MORGINS**. In addition to the above, I would mention Morgins, which I do not know personally, but of which I have heard a good deal. Morgins is 4,406 feet above the sea, and is particularly well-known for its rinks, which seem to be first-class. The skiing is said to be good but not extensive. There is no railway.

**DIABLERETS**, 3,849 feet above the sea, in a valley going from Aigle among the mountains to the East, might be a good centre for skiing, but I only know it in Summer. So far as I have heard it offers the usual attractions in Winter, but there is no railway to help much.

In other districts of Switzerland the following places should be mentioned, although I have never been to them in Winter time.

**ENGELBERG**, 3,343 feet above the sea, in the Stans valley near Luzern, is often well spoken of as a Winter centre, though it is liable to thaw and shortage of snow. From what I know of it in Summer time I should think that most of the surrounding slopes are too steep and precipitous to allow of much free running, but the Titlis group probably provides some open country and there is a short funicular above the village.

There are excellent hotels, and all the usual attractions are offered.

**ANDERMATT**, 4,738 feet above the sea, lies in the Gothard Valley above the Tunnel, and is easily reached in Winter by express trains stopping at Goeschinen, whence a short mountain railway runs up to Andermatt.

I have only been there in Summer, and from what I saw should imagine that Andermatt was subject to a great deal of wind. The slopes all look somewhat steep and are bare of forest, so that they might be somewhat dangerous on account of avalanches.

There is no railway to help Ski runners, but Andermatt might offer quite a lot of good runs to experienced people.

I know nothing of the other attractions for the all-round Winter sportsman, but have little doubt that Andermatt, which is a go-ahead place, does all it can to satisfy them.

There are, of course, innumerable other places which may be good skiing centres, not only in Switzerland, but also in Germany, Austria, and the Italian Tyrol.

The Jura mountains and places, such as Splugen and Schuls in Graubunden, might open up new districts. There is much new country to explore, and I have only picked out for notice the few places to which I have been myself, or of which I have heard from people I trust.

My description may not always be appreciated by people who have special affection for any one centre, but I have only tried to put forward my own impressions for the guidance of any beginner who may feel in a quandary as to what place to choose.

So much depends on weather conditions: if there is plenty of snow and if the sun shines, almost every place is delightful. If, on the other hand, a thaw settles in or fog descends on the mountains, or a blizzard blows the snow about, or, worst of all, if rain falls, reducing the snow to slush, nobody will be satisfied anywhere. Luckily for Ski runners, even a few inches of wet snow will provide practice, so that they suffer less than other Winter sportsmen when the weather is unfavourable.

One thing can invariably be depended upon in Switzerland, namely a warm welcome from the hotels, and every endeavour made to ensure the comfort and enjoyment of their clients.

No country in the world lays itself out more for the satisfaction of its visitors, and no holiday can beat a Winter holiday among the Alps when the conditions are favourable and the sportsmen determined to enjoy themselves.

# CLOTHING

Clothing should be light, smooth, warm, loose and, when buttoned up, it should leave no gaps. It is better to wear several thin, warm garments than one thick one, for the simple reason that going uphill one wants to peel to the minimum; sitting on top of a mountain or ridge in a wind, one wants to pile on everything one possesses, and going downhill one wants a medium amount, all of which will button up so that the snow cannot penetrate inside. Ordinary country clothes will usually suffice for the first season, especially if they are of smooth material which will shake off the snow.

Men usually wear smooth wool or cotton gaberdene coats, and trousers, and a peaked "Guide's" cap. Their trousers either tuck inside the uppers of their boots and should be sufficiently long to do so without pulling out in a strained turn or fall, or they may be buttoned round outside the boots or folded and tied on with Norwegian puttees or swanks. Breeches and stockings may be worn, but long puttees should be avoided as they constrict the muscles and stop the circulation, thus tending to frost-bite, which is a serious danger at high altitudes.

Sweaters, unless worn under a coat when practising or running downhill, are quite unsuitable as the snow gets into the stitches and then melts, and the sweater becomes a sponge and often stretches till it is more like a woman's coat-frock than anything it was before! A skiing suit should be well provided with pockets, all of which should have flaps to button over and keep the snow out. Also to keep the contents in. Money and other things carried loose are apt to fall out in a downhill fall. Once this winter, when getting up from a fall, I saw what looked like a useful leather boot-lace lying in the snow. I picked it up and found it was the bootlace attached to two stop-watches, which I had been using for a test. As one cannot tie one's money up with a boot-lace, it is wise to carry it safely, and cheat the goatherds, who may surely make a profitable living out of the various treasures lost by Ski-ers, which appear on the slopes after the snow melts.

Women need very much the same sort of clothing as men. Either trousers or breeches, whichever they prefer. These should be made to measure in order to fit well and be worn with braces to pull them up. Thick boys' stockings should be worn to pull up over the breeches. If women would only realize how sloppy their nether garments sometimes look and how really horrid breeches look hanging loose over silk stockings indoors, they would surely be more careful to study and copy a man's neat legs before they venture into man's apparel.

One sometimes sees women's coats made with innumerable fancy buttons or tabs as decoration. These only add to the weight which no one would want to carry, and also look out of place. So does fur trimming. Skiing clothes cannot be too simple. Elaboration is easily obtained by bright-coloured gloves, scarves or swanks.

Coats should be made with a belt, which can be buckled tight before the descent. A sitting fall in soft snow is apt to provide the runner with a good dose of snow inside the coat. For the same reason breeches and trousers should be cut somewhat high above the waist.

Women need just as many pockets as men, and I strongly advise two large side pockets and two smaller breast pockets outside the coat, as well as two inside breast pockets—all with flaps to button over.

A felt hat is now usually worn by women Ski runners, who find the brim a comfort on sunny days, while it also protects the eyes when skiing through a blizzard. Incidentally it helps to prevent snow from going down the neck in a head-first fall. A chin-strap may be required for fast running.

Boots are, perhaps, the most important part of a Ski runner's outfit. They must be water-proof and large enough to hold two pairs of socks in addition to stockings. The soles must be so stout that they will not buckle or bend under the instep when the Ski binding is tight. Heels must be low and should be slightly grooved at the back to hold the binding. I have no hesitation in saying that most of the skiing boots sold in England prove to be unsatisfactory. Such firms as Lillywhite and Fortnum & Mason, which make a study of suitable equipment, may be trusted, and almost every Swiss bootmaker now sells trustworthy boots for skiing. I always buy my own boots from Och, who has shops at Geneva, Montreux, Zürich and St. Moritz. They can be relied on for at least two or three long seasons, if one is careful to oil the uppers with boot oil occasionally, and never to oil the soles except with linseed oil, which is said to harden them. On the whole, however, the soles are safest left untouched. Boots should never be dried on a radiator or by a fire. Personally I like hooks, rather than eyelets, and I find that leather boot-laces last longer than others.

There is much discussion as to whether Ski boots should have nails in the soles or not. They tend to wear away the aluminium or linoleum plates fixed to the Skis under the foot, but on the other hand they are almost indispensable when Skis are carried across a hard, steep slope, or down an icy path. It seems to me that it is positively dangerous to go any real Ski tour with unnailed boots unless crampons or spikes to fit on to the heels be carried. New plates can easily be fitted to the Skis when nails have worn through them, but nothing can help the Ski-er down a steep, icy path or across a hard frozen slope on smooth soles, unless he carries special contrivances to fix to his boots.

People are now trying crepe rubber soles, but they are not solid enough to bear the strain of tight bindings unless fixed to the usual thick leather sole, when the whole becomes too thick for comfort. My experience for several winters with beginners is that the soles of most English boots buckle as soon as they are subjected to the tight pull of a leather binding.

Few things are more irritating to a beginner than to find that his binding will not hold on his boot. Over and over again in a run down his Ski comes off and he delays his party by having to stop and put it on again. Still it will not hold even though he ties it on with string. Then he realizes that his boot is buckling. The sole arches up under the instep and the binding, becoming loose, slips off the heel.

There is no cure for this, and the only solution is to use a toe binding, such as the new B.B., or a solid binding such as the Ellessen or Lilienfeld, instead of a heel binding. As most hired Skis have the Huitfeldt heel binding it is essential to ensure that boots are of the very best.

Gloves are another very important item of clothing. They should be waterproof. This is easy to say but very difficult to obtain. The rub of the stick on the palm of the hand tends to sodden almost any material. Snow also gets inside during a fall and then, of course, even the waterproof glove comes home wet. The best gloves are paws made of thick horsehide and lined with wool. They should have long gauntlets wide enough to pull up over the sleeves and they should be joined by a string going round behind the neck, under the coat collar, long enough to allow of free use of the hands, and this string should have another string joining it across the chest. It is often necessary to slip off a glove and if they are not safely hung round the neck they fall in the snow, which promptly runs inside, or they may be dropped and lost.

Socks are a matter for individual choice. Some people like goat's-hair socks, which have many of the qualities or disqualities of a hair shirt. They are prickly and, therefore, perfect as a counter-irritant under very cold conditions, but far too irritating for ordinary wear. I was much amused in a London shop last winter when I heard a skiing expert advising a lady not to buy "those repulsive goat's-hair socks." When she had bought what he advised I said I had come especially to buy "a repulsive pair of socks." He immediately explained that he had advised the lady not to get them because they only had two pairs left, and he did not want to sell them. He let me have a pair, and the only time I wore them I thought with amusement of his advice and explanation. The lady was undoubtedly well out of them, and I hope never to use them again. Some people swear by them, so all tastes must be allowed for.

It seems to me better to wear two thin pairs of socks in addition to stockings, rather than one pair of thick socks. If these seem to fill the toes of the boot too much, the toe part of one pair of socks can be cut off, the remainder being worn as an anklet.

Swanks, or Norwegian puttees, may be used to tie the socks above or over the boot so as to prevent the snow from getting inside. Or shooting anklets may also be used, granted that they are large enough to go over the wide uppers of a Ski boot as well as the socks.

Footgear for skiing is not elegant, but as every one wears the same, nobody need feel shy. It is another reason for buying in Switzerland. Ski boots of the right size bought in a London shop look so Gargantuan that people will often insist on having a smaller pair than is really useful when the time comes to wear them.

Spare clothing should invariably be carried on any run beyond the nursery slopes as, in case of an accident and delay in fetching help, a runner who is hurt may be badly frost-bitten. This, of course, only applies to high places during the months of December, January and early February, when the thermometer may often register 32° of frost or more after the sun goes down.

When choosing equipment it is wise, therefore, to remember spare clothing, which should include a Cardigan or Jersey, a dry pair of woollen gloves, a dry pair of socks or stockings, a warm cap of some sort to cover the ears and a scarf. All these should be chosen for a combination of warmth and lightness. A wind-jacket is often recommended. Some people carry a thin silk, or oil silk, or even chamois leather, or paper waistcoat, to put on under their coats when a wind blows. This is not necessary for any but long tours in midwinter. A very useful "sail-cloth coat" specially made for skiing can be bought in most Swiss sports-shops and is excellent.

The great thing to remember about clothing for skiing is that climbing uphill you will probably get very hot and perspire freely. To stop in a biting wind in this condition without putting on spare clothing is obviously risky. It is difficult to ski freely in heavy thick clothes, so that everything should be warm and loose and made of wool except, perhaps, the wind-jacket or the Swiss coat, which can be worn over a sweater.

Cotton or linen underclothing will probably soon be discarded, but this is a personal matter, and need not be dealt with here.

# EQUIPMENT

The minimum amount of equipment should be purchased before going out. The Swiss shops are just as well provided with skiing necessities as the British and it is expensive to take out heavy luggage. Most Swiss hotels will gladly store Skis or gear of any kind through the Summer, and these can be posted or forwarded by rail to any place the runner chooses for the following season.

Clothing has been dealt with in a former chapter. Here I propose to describe the equipment which I know, from experience, to be useful.

Skis can be bought in England or in Switzerland. One or two English firms, such as Lillywhite, which really take pains to obtain the best possible quality of goods, may be trusted to provide Norwegian Skis, but there are also several makers of good Skis in Switzerland. Skis should be made either of hickory or ash. Other woods such as birch and walnut have been tried but these do not appear to make as satisfactory Skis as hickory or ash. Hickory is heavy so that the beginner will do well to get ash Skis in the first instance. Their average length should be the height of the Runner with his arm extended above his head, the tip of the Ski when standing upright being in the palm of his hand and his fingers just able to bend over it. When the novice becomes more proficient, he may like to try longer or shorter Skis, but the average length is best to begin with.

Good makers, such as Bjornsted in Bern or Staub at Zurich, may be trusted to make their Skis right proportionately, and the buyer need not worry about their width or depth so long as the length is right. There is a great deal of difference in the line of a Ski, as there is in a boat. Flat ones are ugly compared with those which hump along the centre, but they are also lighter. It seems to me wise for the beginner to hire his first Skis, rather than to buy them. Most of the sports shops in the different centres are very obliging and will allow their clients to try two or three pairs of Skis in order to experience the difference between them.

They should not curve up too abruptly in front and they should be about one inch apart in the centre when laid flat one against the other. This spring adds greatly to the comfort of running and should be maintained by the Ski having a block of wood between them when put away for the Summer or even when laid by for two or three days.

The question of binding is a very serious one. Broadly there are three different types:

(1) Toe bindings, by which only the toe of the boot is attached to the Ski.
(2) Solid binding with a sole attached to the Ski.

(3) Leather heel bindings.

(1) I have tried two forms of toe bindings—the B.B. and the B.B.B. and gave them up for the following reasons. Firstly, I think it a dangerous binding. There is practically no give at all so that in a bad fall when the foot is twisted under one, if the Ski does not move the leg has to give way and may be broken. I think surgeons agree that there are more accidents as a result of wearing a B.B. binding than any other—so that it seems to me much better to start with another type of binding and then go into the B.B. later if preferred. Another drawback is that as the whole pivotal pressure in a turn is borne by the toe iron, when a B.B. binding is worn, the toe irons are always being forced open. Not only that, but the spring on the Ski which holds the hook on the boot is so strong that it tends to pull the boot through the toe irons, so that gradually the boot gets longer and more pointed and the spring no longer holds.

All this criticism may be due to prejudice on my part, but I have tried the B.B. with enthusiasm and only gave it up because I was convinced that a heel binding was more satisfactory. Since I tried it, two or three new forms of toe binding have been put on the market, the simplest of which seems to me to be the Davos form, which is merely a strap fixed to the Ski with an iron loop at the end to fit into the hook on the boot and an ordinary Huitfeldt spring buckle to fix it firmly.

(2) Solid bindings. The commonest forms of these are the Ellesen, Lilienfeld and Bilgeri, but as I have never tried any of them, I can say nothing about them.

(3) Heel bindings. There are two main forms of these—the Lap thong and the Huitfeldt. The Lap thong is merely a long strap of raw hide or leather. A loop is drawn through the hole under the toe iron, the long end is taken round the heel and through the loop, then back round the heel and through a slit in the other or short end. The long end is then carried under the foot and round the instep and finally tied off with a knot. This has been improved upon by a ring and buckle being added to save slitting the leather or knotting the ends.

The Huitfeldt binding is a thick double-leather strap, which buckles round the whole foot and has a strong spring to pull it taut when the binding has been slipped on to the heel. This is the usual binding on hired Skis.

I have tried both these bindings, and now wear a Scheer binding, which is a combination of the two—the long Lap thong with buckles and also a spring similar to the one tightening a Huitfeldt binding. The chief drawback to a Lap binding was that it took time to put on so that fingers got very cold and clumsy when fitting it before a run down from a height.

The trouble about a Huitfeldt binding is that it is thick and clumsy and the buckles stick out so that they catch in the snow when running.

The Scheer binding avoids these drawbacks. It is put on just as easily as a Huitfeldt and the thin thong lies so closely along the boot that there is nothing to catch in the snow. It is very easily lengthened or shortened when the leather contracts or stretches and this is also a great comfort. This binding being new, may not yet be obtainable everywhere, but it is well worth trying to get. The Huitfeldt and Scheer bindings both tend to give a little in a strained fall, so that the foot slips round and the leg is usually saved.

Toe irons pass through the Ski under the toes and come up either side to hold the foot in place. They should be carefully fitted and, with a view to this, the boots should be left overnight with the sports shop and the Skis fetched next day. The boot should lie quite straight along the Ski. If the toe irons do not fit properly, the boot will be cock-eye on the Ski, and too much free play may take place. I have often seen beginners take advantage of this to stick their heels out and off the Ski into the snow to help them uphill, or to act as a brake downhill. They will rue it downhill, however, as the foot should be firmly held on the Ski or control will be impossible.

Toe irons are sometimes made of very soft metal. These are usually attached to Skis hired out by the sports shops in order that they may be easily fitted to the many different shaped feet of the hirers. When getting toe irons fitted to one's own Skis, it is wise to ask for strong ones, as the soft irons give too freely to the pivotal action of the feet in turns and tend to be constantly opening and becoming loose.

Cast-iron toe irons are often used in conjunction with toe bindings in order to avoid the difficulty of the irons being forced open by the boot being pulled through by the spring. These irons have one great fault. They have to be screwed on to the Ski and are very cold under the foot. This may be considered imagination, but I believe it to be true, in which case it may be prejudice.

The toe irons are joined over the toes by a leather toe-strap pulled through and buckled. The irons should be so high that this strap does not press at all on the boot, or restrict the free play of the toes. The whole binding should be so fitted that it is possible to kneel down on one's Skis.

Foot plates are nailed on the Ski under the foot. These are usually made of linoleum or aluminium. I prefer a thick plain aluminium plate, and find that the snow does not stick to it.

When the Skis have been chosen, sticks have to be provided. A pair of sticks should be used, one being carried in each hand. They are usually made of hazel or bamboo. The latter are light, but tend to split. I always use hazel, which are cheaper and very satisfactory.

Sticks should be so long that they reach to just above the waist and should not be very heavy though strong sticks are necessary for all real touring. They should have padded leather knobs at the tops, as these prevent the stick from slipping out of the hand and being dropped during a run, as well as saving the hand from blisters when the stick is much used in practising lifted stem or jump turns. Wooden knobs are often used but these tend to get coated with ice, which wets the glove and is uncomfortable.

A leather or webbing thong is passed through the stick or nailed under the knob as a loop to hang them up by, but should never be put round the wrist except for uphill work as the wrist might easily be broken in a bad fall, if the stick be attached to it. My great idea is to get rid of my sticks in a fall, as I once impaled my leg on the spike of my stick in a somersault. I was thankful that the spike was a short one and not one of the newfangled aluminium spikes which would have penetrated much further and might easily have done damage to the bone. Only a short spike is necessary—just long enough to go into crusted snow and hold.

The discs round the bottom of sticks should be large, about seven inches in diameter, and they should be loose so that they will lie flat with the Ski when packed. I prefer them put on with a thong which passes through the stick and is crossed backwards and forwards across the disc, allowing of plenty of free play in the disc. By this means, the thong does not cut where it passes through the stick. Discs are often made almost solid and then fixed to the stick with an iron hasp, which is apt to snap or to split the stick.

Sticks hired out with Skis usually have small discs and no knobs, and most beginners will soon wish to possess their own pair, which only cost about twelve francs. A word of advice here. Keep your sticks in your bedroom. Even in the best skiing circles sticks sometimes disappear—and once your own sticks go, you are tempted to take anybody else's and so the mischief goes on!

The Rucksack is a very important item of equipment It should be waterproof and large, even if you do not intend to carry much. Nothing is more uncomfortable than a small full Rucksack, perching like a football on one's back. By the time a packed lunch and a cardigan as well as some spare gear is stuffed into the sack, it swells. Two outside pockets and one large inside division are indispensable. Keep wax, scraper, string, etc., in one outside pocket ready to hand. Map in the other.

Leather shoulder straps are the best as they do not cut the shoulder in the same way as webbing. I once hunted a great many London shops in vain for a Rucksack with leather shoulder straps. They all had thin webbing, which soon turns into a wisp and hurts the muscles of the shoulder. The leather straps should finish on a ring at the top which should be attached to the top of the Rucksack by a leather tab firmly sewn on. This is a much safer system than running the string, which pulls up the top of the sack, through the shoulder straps at the back, because the pull on the string chafes it and gradually cuts through it. Some experienced runners prefer the Bergans Rucksack on an aluminium frame. It is unquestionably heavier than the ordinary sack, but the frame resting on the hips helps to distribute the weight and it is said to be less tiring to carry. Another joy about it is that the frame keeps the sack off the back, so that there is an air space, and the usual poultice effect of an ordinary Rucksack is avoided.

There are many different types of Rucksack to be had in Switzerland. They should be waterproof and as the waterproof material is very expensive now, a good serviceable sack costs at least Frs. 17.00 to 25.00. The better Rucksacks have straps fixed outside for carrying one's coat or possibly sealskins. (Sohms skins should be carried inside the sack.) I advise people to carry the various contents of their sacks in different bags, or tied up in handkerchiefs. This may sound old-maidish, but it is a trick I learnt from Swiss climbers and I am very thankful. Anyone who has hurriedly searched his sack for some particular bit of gear knows the sort of haystack which results, while if first-aid equipment, sealskins, spare bindings, emergency rations, mending outfit, etc., are all carried in separate, differently coloured bundles inside the sack, endless time is saved. This is particularly worth considering in a blizzard, when fingers are cold and nothing can be found.

Skins are used for climbing uphill on tour. They consist of long strips of sealskin, which are attached to the running surface of the Skis. The hairs lying towards the back of the Ski catch in the snow and prevent the Skis from slipping backwards, which is a great help and saving of energy. The Skis can be kept in good slipping condition with oil or wax, and when the skins are taken off at the top of a run, very little further preparation is necessary.

There are two forms of sealskins:

(1) Sohms skins, which are attached to the Skis with wax.
(2) Those made up on canvas with straps to fix them to the Skis.

The latter can usually be hired by the day for about Frs. 3.00 from the local sports shop, and cost about Frs. 20.00 to buy. Most runners now use the Sohms skins, the great gain being that one can run downhill almost as well when they are still on, so that on a tour with one or two short descents *en route*, the Skis may be left on.

Waxes are of many kinds, and some runners, not content with what they buy, prefer to mix their own.

The waxes most used in Switzerland are Skiolin, both hard and soft, Sohms' with red, yellow or green label, and Parafine.

I have found that hard Skiolin ironed into the running surface of the Ski with a hot iron, provides a good surface. Sohms' wax being a climbing wax is apt to stick to some kinds of snow and if Sohms' skins have been used, it is wise to scrape all this wax off before the run down and to polish the Ski with Parafine wax if it needs a finish. On hard snow this is not necessary.

Some waxes are used as climbing wax instead of skins, but as different sorts are needed for different types of snow, they complicate life almost more than is worth while.

A very good permanent surface on Skis is obtained by oiling them repeatedly with linseed oil, allowing them to dry thoroughly between each coat of oil. This is a somewhat lengthy process and an impossible one if the Skis are in daily use, but it is much the best method at the beginning or end of the season.

The best Sohms' skins are dark grey or black and they cost about Frs. 25. The leather surface should be carefully waxed with green label Sohms' wax before starting on an expedition. The wax should be very thinly spread, and it is wise to get this job done at leisure overnight and to lay the skins together with their waxed surfaces touching, and to keep them in a warm room, but not near a heater or stove.

When starting on an excursion wear the skins wound round your body under your coat so that they remain warm and supple until required. Then wax the running surfaces of the Skis with yellow label Sohms' wax as sparingly as possible. It should be spread smoothly and without lumps. When putting on the skins lay them along the Skis from the tip towards the back and run your thumb down the line of the centre groove in the Ski, while you press the skin on evenly over the whole Ski.

New skins are apt to shrink after use, so it is better not to cut the strap, which slips over the tip of the Ski. The best plan is to make a second slit in this strap and slip it on, and then if the skin is still too long turn the end part up over the Ski at the back, sticking it on with wax. Then, when the skins have been used for two or three days, it is easier to decide what length the strap should be.

Having put your skins on, lay the Skis flat on the snow so that the skins will freeze on.

Sealskins must never be dried by a heater or stove as the heat shrivels them and they are ruined.

When not in use, they can be kept rolled up in a bag and should be carried in the Rucksack rather than hanging on outside. Frozen skins are very difficult to attach.

A scraper should invariably be carried when skiing, even on the Nursery slopes. These are made of aluminium and the best type has a groove which will fit into the groove of the Ski and scrape this as well as the flat surface, as ice is apt to adhere there also. Some runners carry, attached to their belt, a Norwegian hunting knife in its case. This is excellent for scraping the Skis and for any purpose for which a strong knife may be wanted, but it always seems to me that it would be a nasty thing to fall on.

A strong ordinary knife should invariably be carried. The Swiss military knife is the best possible as it seems to include practically everything necessary. A really good one costs about Frs. 12.00 or Frs. 14.00, though inferior steel may be had for a great deal less. It should have a ring and be attached to the belt.

Dark spectacles or goggles should be included in equipment.

A mending outfit is often needed, and at least one member of every party going on tour should carry something with which to mend broken Skis. There are many patterns of spare Ski tip on the market, all of which may be useful in certain circumstances, but I have no doubt that the wooden Ski tip is the best. It is just an ordinary front part of a Ski, about two feet long and planed off, so that it will lie close to the broken Ski. This is fixed on by metal clamps, which are made on purpose and can be bought in most winter sports shops. Holes, at different intervals fitting the clamps which should be put on lengthwise, may be bored beforehand in the Ski tip, in order to save time when the tip may be needed on tour. The gimlet supplied with the clamps is usually a poor one, and I always carry a spare gimlet, a little larger than is necessary, as it is difficult to make the holes in exactly the right place in a broken Ski. Cold and clumsy hands have always to be reckoned with when skiing.

The clamps being somewhat roughly made are apt to break so that one should carry at least five pairs. In putting them on, take care not to drop the little square nut off the bolt into powder snow as it sinks at once and may be irretrievably lost.

Other makes of spare Ski tips include one made of cast aluminium produced by Lillywhite, who will probably improve upon it, as at present it seems to me to be too flat. The method of fixing it is, however, a good one.

The Swiss sports shops also keep light tips made of tin and copper, which are affixed by various methods, but they are usually too short and thin to be more than a makeshift.

If a Ski is broken near the front, the wooden Ski tip, when properly adjusted enables one to run any distance quite comfortably and even permits of turns. It is clumsy to carry except in a Bergans Rucksack. A long, narrow pocket might be sewn diagonally across the back of an ordinary Rucksack in which to carry it, but I am afraid it would be uncomfortable. I tried such a pocket vertically and found it quite intolerable and even dangerous in some falls.

Mending outfit must also include a spare binding and a toe strap, as well as some string and cord, wire, and two or three leather boot-laces. The best spare binding to carry is a Lap thong, as it is easier to push through than a Huitfeldt, unless a thin single strap is carried for the front part of the latter. In any case a bit of wire facilitates the pulling through of the thong or strap.

An inexperienced runner, who has not used a Lap thong, should try fitting one at home before depending on it in emergency, as it is a little tricky to put on at first.

Runners going any distance on tour should carry some sort of first-aid equipment. It need not be elaborate, but should include bandages, a clean dressing (a first field dressing is the best and most compact), iodine and adhesive plaster, and some vaseline or boracic ointment. Even a scratch will go on bleeding on a cold day and be very tiresome. Accidents are miraculously few and far between in skiing, considering the falls and the large number of people who ski. But they happen occasionally, and it is as well to be prepared.

The list of gear could be prolonged to any extent, as "What to carry in my Rucksack" becomes an enthralling hobby. Everyone will eventually decide what he thinks he ought to have, in order to come home with a free conscience after any eventuality. Another runner has suggested my adding a pair of small pincers, a pocket tool outfit, matches or fusees, an electric torch, scissors.

Weight has to be considered, as the more the Ski runner carries the greater the effort, but there is undoubtedly great satisfaction in feeling that one has everything which might be helpful in any emergency. If three or four runners are going together the whole gear can be distributed among them, but this makes it more necessary than ever for the party to keep together as a spare Ski tip or similar luxury is no use at the bottom of a run when the accident is near the top.

Even if one does not need all the gear oneself, it seems better to be prepared to help other people who are in difficulties.

The following lists show firstly what I think every runner going several miles beyond home ought to carry; and secondly what a great many runners carry in addition:

(1) A strong knife with corkscrew, leather punch, tin opener, etc.
(2) A Ski tip, gimlet and mending outfit.
(3) Wire.
(4) String and cord.
(5) Spare binding and toe strap.
(6) Dark yellow glasses (Triplex are safest).
(7) Siren or strong whistle.
(8) Emergency ration of some sort, such as chocolate, raisins, dates.
(9) Spare clothing including cardigan or sweater, dry gloves, dry socks, scarf, cap to cover ears.
(10) First-aid equipment.
(11) Map.
(12) Wax and scraper.

Some runners carry all these things and the following besides:

Matches, lantern (folding), or electric torch, aneroid, compass, pincers, hammer, brandy, thermos with some hot drink.

A great many people will laugh at me for suggesting all this gear, but I do so out of experience. When one has ski-ed some years with a good many people, one looks back with amusement to the number of times when one has been asked to provide any of the above.

People go out without spare clothing, food, first-aid equipment, repair outfit. Something happens, and they at once look round to see where they can borrow. Now borrowing is not part of the game and every runner should be independent. It is easy when going on tour, to divide up the gear so that every member of the party carries his share; it is not necessary for each member to carry the whole of what I have shown. Let each carry enough to feel self-reliant, and let the party carry enough not only for their own needs, but also for any other runner in distress whom they may come across. Skiing should be an unselfish sport.

At a certain centre one Winter, word was brought in at about 3.30 p.m. by a member of a party of three that one of his companions was lying in the forest about a mile away with a badly broken leg. Three runners dashed off from the Nursery slopes with the man who brought the news, to show them the way. I posted a friend to watch where they entered the wood, while two other strong runners fetched clothing and hot drinks in a thermos. Somebody else called up the Rettung chef and the doctor. All this help was mobilized within an hour.

Meanwhile the man was lying in the snow in the wood with a badly broken lower leg. The sun had set and the temperature very low. Not one of the party had any spare clothing or gear of any sort. A sensible man, who had been one of the first three to go off from the slopes told me afterwards that if hot drink and clothing had not come soon, he was convinced that the man would have died. As it was he was nearly unconscious and his pulse had nearly stopped.

Dark came on and the doctor and the ambulance sledge did not arrive. Instead of going the way the others had disappeared, they tried a route they thought easier and took too high a line in the forest. The trees muffled sound, and though both parties were shouting and whistling, they heard nothing till at about 6.30 p.m. one of the watchers heard a runner near and went off after him in the dark and luckily found him. This man was scouting for the doctor and sledge and finally brought them to the scene of the accident at 7 p.m.

By this time some one or two of the watchers had gone home nearly frozen, leaving all possible clothing on the injured man. Three others stayed and rubbed him without intermission, which probably saved his life and limbs. The doctor had brought a splint which he put on by light of an electric torch and the man was taken to the station and sent off at once to the hospital.

Now, all this happened within a mile of home where help was handy. Such accidents happening several miles from home may have far more serious consequences, and every Ski runner, who scoffs at the precautions of people more fussy than themselves, may very likely have the life or limb of someone else on their mind when, had they been a little more fussy, they might have saved it.

Not only that, the selfish runner, who travels light, may well be a serious burden to others and risk their safety and comfort through his own foolhardiness.

Skiing is a game which sorts people out, and where the character of people like sailors, who know what it is to face the elements, shows up well against the civilian, whose greatest risk in life at home is crossing a street at a busy hour.

People may ski for years without getting hurt, and the experienced runner probably hurts himself less than the beginner. Yet it is the experienced runner who carries the gear, the beginner it is who usually scoffs and takes risks, not only to himself, but to the people who have to go out to look for him when he is benighted or hurt.

# CARE OF EQUIPMENT

Skis call for a good deal of attention if one takes the game seriously. People who only come out for a fortnight and who hire any pair of Skis, which they treat as they would the floor of an omnibus, have no appreciation of how much attention Skis need, if they are to be really dependable in all sorts of snow.

New Skis should be well-oiled with two or three coats of Linseed oil, which should dry between each coat. I think hickory needs the oil just as much as ash, but some people disagree with this. The oil hardly goes beyond the surface of the wood and soon rubs off on hard snow, but it preserves the wood as well as giving a slipping surface so long as it lasts. Newly oiled Skis when dry need very little further attention for a few days, as they will run well over all sorts of snow.

When there is no time to oil, because the Skis are in daily use, wax can be ironed in. Most good sports hotels now provide a bench with an electric iron in a special heated and lighted room where the Ski-runner can work happily after tea, or on a snowy day. If no such room be provided, it should be clamoured for, because the waxing of Skis is a much more difficult job without it. The patent iron "Para" is helpful where no electric iron is provided. "Para" is an oblong perforated metal box with a handle which screws in. A lump of Meta (solid spirit fuel) is lighted and put inside and the iron becomes hot and is rubbed up and down the Ski, while wax is pressed against it and dribbled on to the wood.

Almost any wax can be ironed in, but I think the hard black "Skiolin" is best for the purpose. Be careful to wax the groove as well as the flat surface of the Ski.

When Skis are put away for the summer, the upper as well as the running surfaces should be oiled or re-varnished in order to preserve the wood.

Leather bindings may be well oiled with special boot oil to keep them supple.

Skis should never be kept in a hot place, as they are apt to warp, but they should be kept dry when put away.

Boots should never be dried by a fire or on a heater, but should be stored in a cool place. They need occasional oiling of the uppers with some sort of boot oil. Dubbin may also be used and is good for filling places, such as between the sole and the upper. The soles should never be oiled, except perhaps with Linseed oil, which hardens the leather. I think the wisest plan is to leave the soles dry, but if snow balls on them they can be waxed with Ski wax. This is often specially necessary on the heel.

If boots be put outside the bedroom every night, the porter will oil them automatically, in most good hotels.

Sealskins should be wrapped up in newspaper and stored in a cool place when put away. Moth will ruin them if left open and heat crumples them, making them useless. A friend told me that when her seal Skis (webbing ones) were ruined by being put near a fire, she recovered them by soaking them in salad oil. She was certainly using them quite happily afterwards.

# THE ELEMENTS OF SKIING

This book does not profess to be in any way a textbook of the technique of skiing. As stated in the preface, my only idea in writing it is to provide an answer to a good many questions which have been asked me every year. Anyone who deals with a great many people knows that there are always some fifty stock questions, which can quite easily be answered by fifty stock answers. What I say in this chapter about the first run will be the barest elements of Ski running.

Beginners should obtain either Arnold Lunn's books, or those of Vivien Caulfield, and concentrate on the theory of turns. I have known two or three novices who, though they had never even seen Skis before, by dint of studying the technique in theory before they came out, were able immediately to apply it in practice. Most beginners find, however, that the moment the Skis start sliding, all theory is thrown to the winds. Instinct of self-preservation prevails and they sit down. Kind friends looking on say, "That was because you were leaning backwards. You must lean forwards." Off they start again, carry out the advice, their Skis stick for some reason and down they go head foremost—the most difficult fall of all to get up from, and the most aggravating.

The great thing is not to do too much the first two days after coming out. The height affects people more than they realize at first, and great energy, due to the bracing air, is often followed by great lassitude. Most people are not in training, and skiing tries the lungs, nerves, and muscles of the fittest as the whole system seems to be brought into play.

A few hours' practice on the Nursery slopes is usually enough for the first two or three days, and if, at the end of the week, the beginner seems to be falling more than when he first began, half or even a whole day off Skis will produce wonderful results in better balance and general fitness.

Having chosen Skis, and ensured that the toe irons and binding fit you, go out to some gentle slope of about 10° with soft snow, if possible.

Set your Skis at right angles to, or across, the fall of the slope before putting them on, because Skis are quite apt to go off alone if pointing down, hill. It is as well to realize this from the first and to adopt the habit of preventing it in the way I suggest, because many a run has been ruined by a Ski descending alone to the valley below, leaving its owner to get home as best he can on one leg. Even if it only goes down some 100 or 200 feet, the friend who goes after it and brings it back often has a good deal to say, and you are lucky if the Ski has not struck a rock or tree and got broken in its independent run. It is no good getting angry on these occasions. I once watched a boy on a distant slope, who had been obliged to descend some hundreds of feet after one of his Skis. When he got hold of it in a temper he started beating it with his stick, and continued doing so till the stick nearly broke.

While on the subject of runaway Skis, I may as well warn you also against a runaway Rucksack. I put mine down at my feet on a steep hard-crusted slope while I took off my coat one day, and the Rucksack started sliding slowly down below us. The party was made up of beginners and we had ropes on our Skis instead of skins so that no one could catch it up till it stopped about 200 feet below us. To add insult to injury at the same time, somebody dropped a 50-ct. bit at the same moment and this danced off down into the valley, racing the Rucksack and beating it hollow.

But to return to the start. The Skis are safely lying across the slope, and you are going to put them on. Put on the lower one first. Never forget this, because it will often prevent a runaway Ski. If the slope is very steep and hard, you should stick the other Ski upright in the snow above you, in order that it may remain well in hand while you put on the first. You will probably find it impossible to put on your Skis with gloves on. If you lay these on the snow, they will undoubtedly get snow inside them. The safest place to put them is one on each stick, stuck upright on either side of you, or tuck them into your belt or pockets.

When you have your Skis and gloves on and everything else is her-metically sealed, you are ready to start sliding or traversing slowly across the slope, before going straight down it. This will give you time to get the feeling of Skis, which are clumsy at first. Slide one foot forward, then the other, but do not lift them. Now try a kick turn and come back across the slopes to the top and face straight downhill. Keep your Skis closely side by side, one foot leading by about twelve inches and push yourself off with your sticks. Try to imagine that the Skis are only a moving staircase and that all you have to do is to stand upright on them and let them do the rest. If your slope is only 10° and there is nothing steeper below you, the Skis won't do much. Indeed in deep snow they may refuse to move at all, in which case try pushing yourself along with your sticks. The great thing is always to want to run faster than you are going and, therefore, only to choose slopes where you feel that you can keep up as fast as the Skis go. It is a mistake to start immediately down such a steep slope that the Skis run away with you. At the same time it is also a mistake not to increase the angle of your slope as soon as you can compete with it.

Stand upright, press the knees together and try to feel that there is a spring in your knees. Let one or other foot lead so that, if the Skis stop, the front foot takes your weight and prevents you plunging forwards and if the Skis suddenly plunge forward, the back foot is equally ready to take the weight and prevents you from sitting down.

Whatever you do, avoid the hideous doubled-up position of a runner, who bends at waist and knees, with feet parallel and far apart, looking like a note of interrogation and leaving what we call tram-line tracks. By his tracks shall a Ski-er be judged!

Look back and see the line you have left. If your two feet have left two tracks with more than six inches apart in soft snow, you must not be contented. In a good track, the two feet should leave one track, but some bindings make this impossible, so that unless you are wearing a toe binding you need not worry about a gap of two or three inches between your feet. This only applies to soft snow running. On hard or crusty snow, it is almost impossible and also dangerous to keep the feet together.

When you have begun to feel at home on Skis, go off to a much steeper slope and try traversing. Choose a slope which has flattish ground below so that you have an easy out-run and nothing to make you nervous.

Remember for your comfort that if you go across a slope leading with the upper foot and with most of your weight on the lower foot—standing upright and, if anything, leaning a little outwards away from the slope, you can traverse across almost any slope without difficulty, so long as it is not too steep for the snow to bear your weight without slipping itself. Nothing is more comforting to a beginner than to realize this. It takes away the feeling of giddiness and gives confidence, but it needs learning and should be practised at once.

The first tendency of Skis on a steepish slope is to point more and more downhill till, finally having intimidated the beginner into allowing them to go their own way, they plunge straight down, and the beginner collapses. To counteract this put more weight on the heel and less on the toes while traversing.

This will push the back part of the Skis down and the front part uphill across the slope and, if done sufficiently, the Skis will stop and you have begun to get some feeling of control when traversing.

Standing upright the inner edge of your Skis will bite into the snow. Try leaning inwards, as you will do by instinct, and you will find your feet slipping away down the slope and you will gracefully recline full length against it. It is exactly the same when walking across a steep grass slope in Summer. Most of the slips are due to leaning towards instead of away from the slopes.

As you get more confidence in your running, try lifting one Ski off the ground as you slide along. Or even take off one Ski and try running on the other; lifting a Ski will often save a fall. For instance if the Skis get crossed, just lift the upper one and put it down beside the other again while running. It is perfectly easy and yet I have known people who, after weeks of practice, dared not lift a Ski off the ground while moving, only because they had never tried it as routine practice.

Whatever you do by way of practice do it first on one foot and then on the other, or you will become a right or left-footed Ski-er and it will take ages for you to feel equal confidence in either foot. This applies especially to turns. Beginners will often go on practising a turn on the right foot, till they can do it and then have to re-learn it completely on the left foot.

Straight running downhill is mainly a question of confidence and balance. As said before, it is better at first to avoid straight running down a steep slope, because the Skis may go so fast that the beginner is quite incapable of keeping up with them and a fall at very high speed is somewhat upsetting and may temporarily shake your nerve.

Choose a low gradient of about 12° or 15° where you can see the outrun which should be on to level ground or even a gentle rise so that the Skis gradually pull up of their own accord. Soft snow is the easiest and confidence may soon be won in this.

Stand upright or bend the knees, but do not bend at the waist. You should feel as though on springs and you want your weight should be well forward over your feet so that you can keep up with the Skis. Standing in tube or bus, facing the way you are going and not holding on to anything is very good practice at home. You will notice that a bus conductor usually gives with the movement of the bus, so that he is prepared for whatever it does. So with skiing. Look ahead and see what the ground is like, and then suit your balance to what is likely to occur as the ground rises or falls. This soon becomes automatic but it needs thinking out at first.

When the snow is hard, practise side slipping, because it will help you out of many difficulties and once you know the feeling of it, you will find that it replaces the downhill side-stepping, which is so slow.

On hard snow, it is possible to go down broadside on by merely standing on one's Skis and turning one's outer or lower ankle outwards and one's inner or upper ankle towards the other, so that the Skis are lying flat on the snow, instead of the edges biting into it. Push off with your stick from the slope above you and weight your heels or your toes according to whether the Skis are sinking in front or behind. Have confidence, keep upright, lean away from the slopes and let your Skis slide and don't blame me if you suddenly slide into a soft patch of snow, which stops the Skis dead and you fall head downwards. This is all in the day's work. If the surface of the snow is uniformly hard you will slip down without difficulty.

Seriously, side slipping is a huge help and should be learned at once. Mr. Caulfield gives first-class instructions, which are easy to follow in detail.

When going uphill never try to climb steeper than is easy. If the Skis are slipping back, you are going too steep and should turn off and traverse instead. No time is saved by too steep a climb; the man who goes easily gets to the top first, while the other clambers up almost on all fours, gets hot and exhausted and has gained nothing. If I am leading an elementary run uphill, I can soon pick out the experienced runners by the line they take and the pace at which they climb. The puffing, panting, stumbling people, who forge ahead, herring-boning or turning their ankles over their Skis so as to get a grip with their boots, are not included in my "experienced runners."

Another hint for uphill work is that when traversing a slope, the Skis should be edged so that the inner edge of the Ski bites into the slope. A Ski with its whole surface flattened to the slope is bound to slip especially on hard snow. By standing upright as you go uphill and keeping the ankles straight, the Skis will be edged in the right way.

A quick way of getting up a steep slope is side-stepping. As you stand with your Skis horizontal across the slope, lift the upper foot and place it on the slope a few inches higher. Then lift the lower foot and place it beside the upper. You will soon be able to do this while advancing across your traverse at the same time, but it is hard work and should only be used for short climbs.

Side-stepping is a very good way of climbing, but should be avoided when descending, except when approaching a narrow gap in a fence or crossing a stream where the approach is steep.

I have known a party almost benighted by a beginner, who had discovered the joys of side-stepping and proposed to descend some 1,000 feet by this safe method, instead of sliding in the proper way. Allowing eight inches to each side-step, how many hours would it take to descend 1,000 feet?

A further hint, which may be useful for uphill work. If the Skis are slightly lifted at every push forward, they tend to stick instead of sliding back.

Always stand upright when climbing and keep the weight well on the heels. People tend to bend forward and this adds greatly to the effort and the Skis are more likely to slip back.

On long climbs sealskins are usually used on the Skis. The hairs lying towards the rear stick into the snow and prevent the back slip, while when the Ski pushes forward, they lie flat and offer no resistance.

The best uphill track is the one which keeps going at the same angle. Every good walker knows how tiring it is to go up and down across country when gullies have to be crossed. It is disappointing, having got up a certain height, to lose all that is gained by going down again. So it is even more with skiing, when uphill work is really more arduous than walking. Mr. Caulfield gives a very helpful description of a good uphill track, and Skis tend to teach the beginner how to keep the angle as they slip so easily downwards the moment the uphill direction is altered.

When going uphill make up your mind what point you want to reach in the distance and what line will take you to it most easily and then go for it steadily, keeping the same angle all the way so far as is possible and choosing your places for turns very carefully before you reach them.

Following an experienced leader teaches a great deal about the art of setting an uphill track, and the criticisms of the rest of the party following, when the leader loses height soon make one want to avoid comment.

# ETIQUETTE

In organized skiing centres a perfectly good code of etiquette is growing up as the result of experience.

So many novices pour out on to the slopes with no knowledge of the game that notices are even posted on the boards in the hotels giving a few of the main points of the Law.

One such notice runs as follows:

(1) Ensure that you take your own Skis, sticks, etc. when you start out. It is wise to mark sticks, and they are safest kept in bedrooms.
(2) Never join a private party unless invited.
(3) Only join the advertised tours, the test for which you have passed.
(4) The slower mover has the right of way. The faster mover must avoid him. Never call "Fore," "Achtung," etc.
(5) Always offer help to anyone in difficulties.
(6) Keep with your party. They might waste a lot of time looking for you while you run home because you thought their pace too slow.
(7) Never desert a runner who, for any reason, is unable to keep up with a party.
(8) Carry your own gear including spare clothing, skiing necessaries, etc.
(9) Avoid stepping on the Skis of another runner. This caution is especially necessary for uphill work.
(10) Remember that wherever you leave a track others may follow. Therefore only choose safe slopes. The snow is liable to slip on slopes of 25° or more, so that these are dangerous.

Skiing is a sport which can be made dangerous for others if individuals do not carry out the usual etiquette. It may seem extraordinary that people should need warning not to join a private party unless invited, but it is sadly true.

One day as I was starting off on a long run a stranger came up to me and asked if she might join us. I consulted the Guide, and he said he already had as many in the party as he could take charge of. I told the lady this, and said I was sorry that we could not accept her companionship. She at once replied cheerily, "Oh, then I will follow you." Nothing could prevent her from doing this. Switzerland is a free country, and there is a right of way anywhere over the mountains in winter. We started off and she followed. From that moment, of course, we automatically became responsible for her because one of the Laws is that you never desert a runner who is alone. She was a very poor performer and fell a great deal, so that for the whole six or seven miles' run, we were kept waiting for her. Of course, we were under no real obligation to look after her, but had we left her and anything had happened to her, we could never again have held up our heads as Ski-ers.

On another occasion a runner made a formal complaint to me about a lady who joined his party. In this case it was an experienced runner, who had presumably learnt the Law, and who might have read the notice on the board. First of all she said, "May I go with you?" and the somewhat cold answer was that the party was complete. Then she followed asking questions about the route, etc. at every opportunity. Of course, she had finally to be adopted and taken along much to the boredom of the party, which was a private one.

Where the skiing is organized, tests are run and tours arranged for the different standards. This does not apply so much to 2nd or 1st-class runners who, of course, prefer to make up their own parties, but, at any rate, these are protected from having the less experienced runner with them, except by invitation. By these means the organized tours only take runners up to the standard advertised, and no one need feel compunction at leaving members of their party behind in the village, because they know that the elementary runner will also get a chance of a run.

Yet even under these arrangements, I have found a beginner sitting huddled in a corner of the railway carriage when we have started before dawn for a big tour. "Where are you off to?" I said, thinking he was out with a Guide. "With your party," was the reply. What could I do? It is not easy to turn a person out of a train at 5.45 a.m. on a cold morning. I said weakly, "Did you not see the notice which said this was a run for 3rd-class runners only?" He said, "Yes, but I thought I could keep up." So there he was, and we took him through and though he was very slow uphill and kept us all back in this case, he ran down without delaying us. People often put their own capacity higher than do the people they want to run with and it is very difficult to be tactful.

Again most people would not think it necessary to warn runners against deserting their party. Yet they often do and it is not usually the beginner who is the culprit here. Perhaps he cannot run quick enough to get away! I shall always remember a run in charge of a tour when I was with a lot of novices. Another experienced runner accompanied me officially to help. I chose what I thought the easiest way to start, and he wanted to try another route at the top and went off saying he would join us below a wood. When we reached the part where I thought we should rejoin, I waited and shouted, but he did not appear. So we went on to another post where we had lunch, and then I began to get anxious as this runner never turned up. Anything might have happened to him. He might have gone over a rock or into a tree or even only be tied up in one of those tangled falls when it is practically impossible to extricate oneself. It was no good our trying to look for him then, so after about two hours' delay, I took my party down to the valley and the first person who met us in the village was our lost companion. He chaffed us for being so late as he had run down very quickly and had had his tea ages ago.

No party going beyond the Nursery slopes should consist of fewer than three. One to go for help in case of need, the other to stay with the third runner, who may need help. Needless to say, people who know the mountains well, go off alone with impunity. When I asked one of these lonely runners what would happen if he hurt himself and was benighted, he told me he always carried sufficient morphia to put him out of his agony in case of need. This was, no doubt, all right from his point of view, but what of the people who might go out to look for him among the infinite possible runs with Ski tracks in every direction.

No sporting runner would ever refuse help to a lame duck, though pretty bad cases of selfishness have been recorded.

There is one point, which does not always strike people, and that is the danger of cutting a track over a difficult place. Beginners will usually follow a track instead of working by their map. For instance on the Muottas Muraigl run at Pontresina, if once a rash runner cuts a track straight across from the restaurant to the valley, crowds will probably follow it, though they may be warned against it. This is a very dangerous slope under certain conditions as was shown this Winter, when a runner going along its top was carried down to the bottom of the valley by the avalanche he started.

I have one track left on my conscience; when a few of us went down what might have been a dangerous place under different conditions to those we found. Luckily it was not a way most people would have wished to follow as it apparently led nowhere and hardly looked attractive.

The slower mover always has the right of way when skiing, so that no runner ought to shout to those ahead of him to get out of his way. Needless to say this does not apply to a runner out of control, who may be dashing unwillingly into someone in front of him when, for both their sakes, a friendly warning is advisable!

It is the business of every Ski-er to avoid obstacles and the slower mover may be looked on as such in just the same way as a rock or a tree. I was amused one day at Pontresina when a crowd of us were going up the village street and met a lady on Skis being held back as she went downhill by two friends on either side of her. It was the first time I had ever thought of someone going down hill being the slower mover in relation to those climbing.

Nursery slopes are for the practice of turns and the individual who uses them for straight running while a lot of people are practising is abhorred. The same applies to jumps on the Nursery slopes. These are so easily made where other people are not practising that it is selfish to come plunging down into a crowd of devotees to turns. When the Nursery slopes are empty, it is great fun to practise straight running down them and no one will object.

One jolly thing about Ski runners is that they seldom ridicule one another or laugh at falls in any but a friendly way. There is great rivalry and daring to greater effort, but ill-natured ridicule is seldom heard. Perhaps this is due to the fact that most people who live in glass houses do not throw stones. Everybody who tries to improve his Skiing is bound to fall and it is better not to set the fashion of laughing at others in difficulties.

There will always be some people who like to look on at tests as "Free entertainment without tax," but if they could hear the comments on their behaviour and probably on their own lack of prowess they would soon give up the habit.

Anyone who is really keen to get on and who will go on practising and accept advice may be sure of sympathy and help. Skiing with all its dangers and need for combined effort seems to bring out the best of people and to produce the very best spirit of goodwill and tolerance.

Going uphill in soft snow, every strong member should take a turn at cutting the track. It is often heavy work, and an energetic leader may not like to ask for help. The best plan is to work by time, the leader falling out at the end of his shift and letting the party pass him till he takes his position at the rear and the second man becomes the leader and so on.

People who are wise, will avoid stepping on the Skis of the man ahead. This is often difficult as instinct makes one want to go faster than the person ahead, just as a wheeler in a tandem will usually try to catch up the leader. The easiest way to avoid overlapping is to keep step. Push forward the right foot, when the man ahead pushes forward his right foot and then the left. This gives a rhythm to the uphill work, which also seems to minimize effort. Anyone who has experienced the irritation caused by his Skis being constantly touched by the runner behind while plodding uphill will learn to spare another the same nuisance.

When running straight down a steep slope make sure that there is no one ahead whom you might run into and no one below on either side, who might traverse across the slope you propose to run down. This is especially necessary in a gap between trees. Another member of your party might be among the trees below and suddenly come out into the open, traversing to the other side. When straight running at any speed, only the best Ski runners can turn suddenly to avoid a difficulty, and a nasty collision may occur if care be not exercised.

When a crowd of people are taking their Skis by train, a great deal of trouble may be avoided in getting the mass of Skis out of the train if these are tied neatly together.

A pair of Skis tied near the tips and behind the bindings is easy to handle, while a pair of Skis put together by slipping one through the toe-strap of the other is a great nuisance.

Skis piled together soon become very like a heap of spillikins if not carefully handled and a good deal of damage may be done to them as well as delay to the train if Ski-ers are careless in this small matter.

Another good plan is for the Ski-ers to form themselves into a queue and to hand out all the Skis along the line, till they can be easily distributed where there is space. The beginner is apt to hunt anxiously for his own pair, which may be at the bottom of the pile, and while he pulls and tugs with but little success, other people are waiting in vain for a chance to get their Skis out. This is especially the case on funicular railways, where space is very limited in the stations. Different nationalities travelling together add considerably to the confusion and the railway officials are usually thankful to anyone who will take charge and get a line formed and the Skis handed out tidily.

These hints may seem unnecessary to a great many people, but no matter. I have had so much of my own time wasted by this sort of tiresome lack of sense that I venture to suggest a means of saving time and temper for others.

Ski runners should remember that sledges and pedestrians have the right of way on a road. All the fields are open to the Ski runner and he should not monopolize a road. In most parts of Switzerland there is a law by which everyone has right of way everywhere where the snow lies—so long as it is not enclosed ground. This was brought home to my family rather vividly, when we lived at Davos, by a shooting gallery being set up on our land in front of our house. We had no power to prevent it and there it remained for the winter. At the same time, Ski runners should respect the property of other people, and here I would like to make two appeals to British runners.

Firstly, that we will do our best to avoid damaging young trees. (Old trees can probably look after themselves where the Ski-er is concerned as they are usually stronger than he is.)

Secondly, that we should treat the inhabitants of the country with as much courtesy as possible. The peasant, over whose land we run, makes very little out of the tourist business and has other things to think about rather than sport. He is usually courteous and friendly and always ready to help us when in difficulties. Let us return his hospitality be treating him with courtesy. School teachers have told me that they have great difficulty in persuading the children to greet foreigners because these so seldom respond. Yet few things are more pleasant than the friendly "Grüsse," or "Grüss Gott," or "Leb wohl," with which one is greeted by the people of the country. We can answer in English if we do not know how to answer in German, but do let us answer and, thereby, prove ourselves as friendly as our hosts.

Another matter, which is not always understood by beginners on the snow fields is that when an Alpine Club or local Ski Club hut is used, a fee should be paid to the funds which support the Hut. These Huts are expensive to build and their upkeep is a great tax on the Clubs. British runners can either join the local Club, when they can use the Huts by day for nothing, or they can pay the advertised fee for whatever use they make of them.

A notice is always posted in the Hut showing the various charges, but when no one is there to collect the money, it is left to the honour of the guests to pay it. A money-box can be found in all huts within Switzerland proper, but as these boxes are not safe from marauders near the frontier, the Ski runner has to send the money in by post. At the Boval hut, for instance, above the Morteratsch Glacier, a supply of money order forms will be found hanging near a door. All the leader of the party has to do is to collect the money from his members, take one of the forms and pay the money into any post office, whence it is sent to the H.Q. of the Club.

Huts should invariably be left tidy. This also is a matter of honour. The doors are unlocked always in order that people who may need hospitality, in case of distress, can find shelter. Blankets can be borrowed. Wood is usually provided for firing and there may even be a reserve of food, all of which should be respected. Before the party leaves, blankets should be folded, shutters should be shut, snow swept out and debris buried outside, or what can be used as fuel put away tidily in the kitchen. Then the door should be shut carefully and the hut left the better, rather than the worse off for having given hospitality.

# SNOW AND LIGHT

Full descriptions of the different types of snow which must be negotiated by the Ski-runner will be found in Mr. Arnold Lunn's book, "Alpine Skiing."

It is only necessary for me, therefore, to describe the four main types, namely, soft, hard, crust and sticky snow.

Soft snow in winter is the new powder snow, which is to be found after a fall or on North slopes where sun and wind have not spoilt it. It is the ideal snow for the luxurious runner, especially two days after it has fallen, when it has settled down and a hard frost has converted it into crystal powder. A run through crystallized snow, which tinkles as the Skis cut through it, is beyond description.

Even a bad runner will find that he can do marvels as the snow seems literally to help him in all his experiments. I have known a day when a blinding blizzard has started blowing the snow into my face and I have run fast along the bottom of a valley with my eyes shut. The Skis kept to the lowest line and ran safely and steadily through this powder snow at a low gradient. It is not suggested that blind running should be indulged in as a rule and I only quote this case to show how helpful is good powder snow.

The Telemark is the usual turn in soft snow. Christiania and jump turns can also be used by people who are proficient and strong, but they require both skill and strength.

Soft snow is usually found on North slopes or at the bottom of shady valleys or even behind any ridge which protects it from the sun or wind. Also among trees which shelter it. Tracks ruin it in time so that it is usually wise to sidle off the track and try new snow beside it.

Luckily for the experienced runner, most beginners usually behave rather like sheep, preferring tracks to exploring on their own. The result is that perfect snow can often be found alongside the beaten track, and when this gets spoilt, it is only necessary to go a little further afield in order to get a good run. Then, as more and more people beat down the track it becomes hard and very amusing running can be had there.

Hard snow is of two types—a beaten track or a hard crust where the sun has melted the surface and the frost at night has frozen it, so that it will bear the weight of the Ski-runner. When this is really solid enough to allow of side-slipping and stem, or Christiania turns, it is very trustworthy and easy to negotiate. At first, however, it intimidates the beginner, because it is very fast. As time goes on and he becomes accustomed to the skid and rattle of hard snow, he will find that his horror turns into pleasure because he can trust it. The Nursery slopes become hard after two or three days and will provide useful experience for coping with such snow on a run.

The lifted stem and Christiania are the best turns on hard snow. A Telemark is apt to skid too much.

Crust is the bugbear of all runners and is out and away the most difficult to tackle. It may be hard, and then with nothing apparent on the surface to warn you, the Skis break through and catch in the crust and down you go. When crust is about, let someone else lead, and then profit by his experience.

There are many forms of crust, all of which may be met on the same run, and when wind has been at work, there may be crust on North slopes and not on South. After rain too, when the surface has been soaked and a frost follows, crust will be found everywhere.

Sticky snow is usually due to the effect of the sun or to Fohn wind or thaw. It is easily coped with by proper waxing of the running surfaces, but the sudden sticking of the skis, which have been running well over wet snow in the open, when they get into cold powder snow under trees or in shadow, is very disconcerting.

The same is apt to happen when people have dried their Skis in the sun by sticking them on end while lunching. The sun not only dries them but warms them so that if the first run after lunch is in shadow and the snow is cold, the Skis stick because the warm surfaces melt the snow, which immediately freezes again and adheres to the Skis, so that they come to an absolute standstill.

The only way to avoid sticking is to keep the running surfaces of the Skis in good condition by oiling them thoroughly and to carry one or two different types of wax for use according to circumstances.

The great thing is to get practice on all types of snow and never to mind it. Look upon crust as a joke, and learn jump turns, which are the only safe turns for any but the strongest runners. Some of these can accomplish a Telemark, or stem-turn or even a Christiania on every sort of snow, but most people are content with the jump turn on crust. The great trouble of this turn is that it is very tiring when a heavy Rucksack is carried, but knack and good use of the stick will help it.

Light is a great factor in skiing. On a fine day when visibility is good, it is easy to distinguish between the rise and fall of country ahead and, therefore, to be prepared for decrease or increase in speed. Some days when the sky is clouded, it is practically impossible to tell what is coming. This difficulty is increased in a narrow valley when the reflection of the slopes on either side make the whole surface look identical.

Coloured glasses may help a little, but it is better to run slowly and to take no risks. On these occasions tracks help immensely as they give the eye something to follow. Rocks and trees also help; anything that breaks the surface of the snow and shows up the gradient ahead.

# FALLS

Falls!—what a word. When I first thought of writing this book, it struck me that the best selling title would be "Skiing without Falls." But then I remembered that I could never look a beginner in the face again if, knowing that he had read my book, I saw him fall.

Besides which, a Ski runner who never falls, is probably but a poor exponent of the sport. When you begin to run comfortably and can do the turns at low speeds, falls show that you are still trying to learn more of the game. It is only by trying new things that a runner becomes really proficient and you are almost certain to fall constantly as you learn. There is art in falling on Skis as well as in running and turning. Fall loose. Let yourself go; never try to save yourself when once you find the fall is inevitable and get rid of your sticks. You will have the most amazing falls on Skis and nobody will listen to your descriptions of them because they are just as eager to describe their own. The surprising thing is how little people hurt themselves—knees and ankles go most. The strain on the knee and ankle is very great in some falls, but if you let yourself go and relax your muscles as you fall, you will find that even ankles and knees survive as a rule.

I once saw a really good runner turn three somersaults while nose-driving down a steep slope at high speed in soft snow. And all the damage done was two hat-pins snapped! Moral, don't wear hat-pins.

People are so tangled up sometimes that they do not know whether the Ski tip sticking out of the snow belongs to their right or left foot, and they have to dig with their sticks before they can extricate themselves. And sometimes the results of a fall are so intricate that the runner could never extricate himself, but needs the help of a friend, who will undo a binding so as to free him. The most curious fall I ever saw was when a man, running down a steep slope among trees, ran into a fir tree on the upper side where the snow was lying well up the trunk. He then fell head downwards into the hole below the tree where the snow had not penetrated and, his Skis being caught in the branches, there he hung. Had he been alone, I doubt whether he would ever have succeeded in getting free. As it was, we undid a binding quickly and no damage was done.

Not only is there art in falling but there is a technique of getting up. Before attempting to get up, arrange your Skis so that they are ready to stand on. Suppose they are crossed below you on a steep slope, lie on the slope, raise the Skis in the air, uncross them, set them parallel across the slope below you, facing the way you want to go, and get up. This fall is sometimes used as a turn and may be very useful, though not considered the best possible form if done intentionally.

Never attempt to get up on to Skis facing downhill. They will only go off with you the moment you begin to rise, and then down you flop again.

If you fall head downwards down a slope, you still have to get your Skis parallel across the slope below you before you can stand up, and the only thing to be done is to turn a somersault uncrossing your Skis in the air if they are crossed and getting them below you and then standing up. All of which is extremely easy, but it is very necessary to ensure that clothes are so made that the powder snow cannot slip into crevices while you are gambolling in this fashion. The first thing I do before getting up from a fall is to put up my hands and let the snow shake out of my glove gauntlets.

If you are so tangled up in a fall that it is almost impossible to get out, just undo a binding, slip off a Ski and get up easily with a free foot to stand on. And, if you see anyone else so tangled up that he does not begin to get up immediately, hurry to his assistance, because his ankle or knee may be in a very strained position and he may be thankful to you for undoing a binding and releasing him. It is in these falls that the leather heel bindings so often prove better than a rigid toe binding. The leather will ease a little or slip and allow the foot to turn a fraction of an inch so that the strain is not maintained long enough to cause real damage.

Falls are often half the fun of skiing, and every runner who is trying something new will sometimes fall in the endeavour. So never lose hope, however much you fall. If you have been running rather well, and then get a day when you do nothing but only means that you are stale and that your muscles and nerves need a rest. This is where the all-round Winter sportsman gains. He can spend a day on the rink or curling or tobogganing and not feel that he has wasted time.

Never scoff at people because they fall. A first-class runner is supposed to be able to run at high speed, using turns without falling. So he will, probably, if he intends to, but no first-class runner worth his salt would always run like this. He will always be trying something more difficult, turns at higher speed or in difficult snow, and consequently he will often be seen to fall, and the beginner who scoffs is merely voted an ignoramus. Here again a runner will be judged by his tracks. Look carefully at the place where he ran and try to make out what turn he was trying and what the snow was like, and why he fell. You can learn a great deal from other people's tracks.

Falls in deep snow are always a little more risky than on hard snow, because there is greater strain on muscles and ligaments. On hard snow you get many a bump and scratch, but the results are less lasting than a torn ligament.

Having got up safely from your fall, look on the snow and see what you have dropped before starting off again. Even pockets with flaps may allow of leakage.

It is wise to tie your Rucksack firmly with a strap round your waist because, if it is loose, anything heavy inside may give you a nasty bump on the head as you fall.

# TESTS

There are three British Ski tests under the Federal Council of British Ski Clubs. In addition to these, different centres and local clubs often set an elementary test for beginners in order that these may be sorted into various standards for expeditions.

Hitherto the Elementary test has usually been a run down a certain distance within a time set by the judges. This is not an altogether satisfactory test, as the beginner, who goes straight down sitting on his Skis may get through, while another, who conscientiously tries to run standing, falls the whole time and fails. Style might be judged and the sitting candidate disqualified, but when, as often happens, some seventy or eighty people enter for an Elementary test, the judges have their hands full enough with starting and timing, apart from watching individual running critically as in the 2nd-class test.

A better way, therefore, is to flag a line, which must be followed, providing traverses across slopes, which soon catch out the sitting novice.

Beginners usually hate traversing because they dislike the look of a steep slope and do not know how to prevent the instinctive pointing straight downwards of the Skis. They do not realize yet that if they would stand upright on their Skis while traversing, and lead with the upper foot while they put their weight on the lower foot and keep their whole weight somewhat on their heels, they will traverse quite easily at a gentle angle.

The Elementary test ought to be so planned as to force this type of running.

Another way of running an Elementary test is for a judge to lead at a steady easy pace for an hour's cross-country run, including both up and downhill, as well as level running and obstacles. The test would be timed, an ample margin being allowed beyond the judge's time. All those, who finished within the time would pass.

This would probably not be nearly so popular a Test with the candidates as the short downhill run, but it would be a far better test of their capacity for touring.

The British Ski tests consist of the 1st, 2nd and 3rd-Class Tests, the Regulations for which will be found in the Ski Year Book, which can be obtained from the Hon. Secretary, Federal Council of British Ski Clubs, Essex Court, Temple, London, E.C. They can also be obtained from any official representative of one of the British Clubs in Switzerland, and are printed as an Appendix at the end of this book.

In the 3rd class test, which is the first and which has to be passed before the runner can go up for his 2nd class, there are three parts.

Part (a) is a climb of 1,500 feet in not more than 1-1/2 hours and a run down 1,500 feet in a time set by the judges. The time may not be less than seven, or more than twenty minutes. It should not be more than 12 minutes under good conditions.

Men must carry Rucksacks weighing not less than 6 lbs., and women 3 lbs. Sealskins may be used for the climb.

Part (b) consists of four consecutive lifted stem-turns on a slope of 15° to 20°, and Part (c) four consecutive Telemark turns on a slope of the same gradient. Parts (b) and (c) are often used as a qualifying test before Part (a) is run, in order to limit the entries for Part (a), which may otherwise be a very difficult test to run when a large field enters for it.

Candidates who enter for this test should really take pains to ensure that their bindings fit their boots and that they have everything necessary for a run as well as being up to the standard. Speaking as a judge of four years' standing, who has run innumerable tests, I may say that it is pitiable to see the number of casual people who will come up for a test without reading the regulations and without being in any way prepared for a 1,500 ft. climb. Few things are more disagreeable than having to disqualify a candidate, who turns up without a Rucksack, or more miserable than having to shepherd down beginners who are worn out by a run for which they are quite out of training. The one comfort is that a candidate, who is pertinacious and courageous enough to face this test five or six times without passing and goes in again, is almost sure to pass in the end.

For the judge's sake, however, I strongly urge such a candidate to time himself over similar runs with his friends and to persist in this until he proves that he is up to 3rd-class standard, when he will be a very welcome candidate in the test itself.

A course is easily found by using an aneroid, or it may also be worked off the Ordnance Map. Any ordinary watch with a second hand will suffice for the timing of one's own run.

Some people may think that I am a little harsh in my reasons for suggesting that beginners should not enter for the running part of the 3rd-class test so lightheartedly. It is really for their own sakes as much as for that of the judge's. Failure is very discouraging, and I have known people's nerve quite upset by one of these runs. They have tried to race down and have taken really nasty tosses in their rush, while the fatigue of constant falling and getting up out of deep snow, becoming more and more out of breath in the anxiety to compete, is very bad for their running. I have often wanted to hide my head in shame when coming home after such a test with a lot of worn-out people, wet through, who have failed. And yet, such is life, that many with the first breath, after they finish exhausted, will ask when the next Test takes place in order that they may compete again. Such a candidate really does one's heart good.

Tests have probably done more than anything else to improve the standard of British running. We all have a liking for competition, and here is our chance. Having succeeded in passing the 3rd-class test, we can wear a badge and then we have to ski better in order to prove worthy of it, and presently we see no reason against qualifying for the 2nd-class test before going home. "After all, the turns only have to be done on a steeper slope." "The run can be put off till next Winter, and passed the moment we come out," they say.

The 1st-class standard is rising higher and higher as British Ski runners become more proficient. The runner who passed a year or two ago now hesitates to wear the gold badge, because he often realizes that his speed and turns are not good enough for what is now required.

Judges of the British Ski tests may be found in most well-known centres, but, as there are very few 1st-class people, the tests for this class are usually run in one or two districts only.

# GUIDES AND SKI INSTRUCTORS

Swiss Guides are certificated by the Swiss Alpine Club and are the only people permitted by law to guide parties among the higher mountains. A tariff exists in every district showing the fees which these Guides must charge. In addition to the fee, the client usually gives a gratuity and also pays for the Guide's accommodation and provisions on the tour. A percentage may be added for numbers greater than those provided for in the tariff, while on a really difficult tour, the Guide will probably refuse to take more than two or three runners unless a second Guide or porter be engaged. The Certificated Guides wear a badge issued by the Swiss Alpine Club and any man wearing this may be depended upon to be a good fellow, a careful Guide, and a philosopher and friend. Most of them can now ski well, though a few of the older ones may not be very proficient in technique and may be stick riders.

When on tour with a Guide, he is responsible for the safety of the party, and every member should do his best to help him by carrying out any instructions he may give for their greater safety. This is not always appreciated by people who do not know the Alps and their unwritten laws, and the Guides complain somewhat bitterly that they are often put in very difficult positions. For instance, on one occasion, when a party was crossing an avalanche slope, the Guide asked them to go singly at intervals of 20 metres, so that if anyone was carried away, the others would not be involved and could go to his rescue. One of the party was overheard saying: "Oh! he is only trying to prove how careful he is in order to get a higher tip," and they were careless in their carrying out of the instructions.

In any case it is discourteous not to do what the Guide prescribes and he is put in a very false position as he is held responsible.

Ski Instructors belong to a different category, unless they are also Certificated Guides, which is often the case. In some Cantons, such as Graubünden, the Instructors have to pass an examination showing their capacity to ski and also to teach. Many of them are perfectly beautiful runners, but they should not be pressed to conduct tours where glacier work or rock climbing is involved. They are not examined for this and they hold no credentials, and if an accident occurs, everyone is blamed. There are a great many other runs they are allowed to lead and they will set as good a course as anyone would wish for.

Before engaging a Guide, or an Instructor on the recommendation of the concierge, get some expert advice as to who is the best. The Secretary of the local Ski Club would advise or some good runner in the neighbourhood.

In some parts of Switzerland the Guides and Instructors have taken to touting for clients. They hang about the hotels and try to induce the unwary to engage them and to go for tours for which they are often not fit. The better Swiss Guides are the first to want the public to discourage this type of behaviour, as it is doing a lot of harm to their good name.

When a Guide is engaged, treat him as a friend and trust him. They are usually a most obliging and reliable set of men, who will do everything in their power for their clients, such as carrying food and spare clothing, waxing skis, attaching skins and even making terms in inns, and cooking the food in huts when on tour. Their knowledge of the mountains and their experiences are well worth probing, and they will usually talk willingly when kindly dealt with. They are quick judges of character and if the younger ones are sometimes a little inclined to take advantage of the people who do not treat them suitably, only those people themselves can be blamed. The old-fashioned Guides are never familiar, though they are very friendly and will always do their best for the entertainment of their party. They should not be petted and flattered, neither should they be treated as inferiors. A happy medium is easily found which is what the Guide will prefer, because in his heart of hearts, he has the whole of the Swiss characteristics—great dignity, independence and respect for wise people.

On a long and dangerous tour the safety of the party may ultimately depend upon the trust and confidence placed in the Guide in charge, and by him in his clients, and this should be remembered in all negotiations. These men often have to risk their lives for the sake of the people who employ them, and their staunch unselfishness is a fine example of human endeavour for the benefit of others. Their fees may appear to be high, but when everything is taken into consideration, including the shortness of their Winter and Summer Seasons, it is soon realized that the fees are not exorbitant.

# MAPS AND FINDING THE WAY

Every Ski runner going across country should carry a map. Even on a short run a great deal can be learnt from a map, which will prove useful later on a longer run. Both time and risk can be saved by people who run by their map and who know how to avoid dangerous places and how to take advantage of narrow safe openings.

There are different types of maps to be had in Switzerland. The best are the official Ordnance Maps published by the Eidg. Landestopographie at Bern. The mountain districts are produced at a scale of 1 centimetre in 50,000 centimetres or 2 centimetres in one kilometre, and large or small sheets can be bought almost everywhere. The gradients are clearly shown by contour lines. The equidistance being 30 metres, or roughly 100 feet, the dotted contour lines when height is marked some every 8 or 10 ordinary contour lines. This differs according to the edition. Cliff and rock are shown grey, while glacier contour lines are blue.

Some districts, such as the Bernese Oberland, have produced this map with red lines showing all the Ski runs. In other places they also provide Skiing maps, but on a different scale and not as good as the Ordnance Map.

All maps are best when mounted on linen, as the weathering they receive on a run may reduce a paper map to pulp or rag.

It is easy to work out the distance of runs or the gradient of slopes from the large scale Ordnance Map. 1 in 50,000 metres means that 1 centimetre on the map equals a run of 50,000 metres; 2 centimetres equal a kilometre or 100,000 metres; 8 kilometres equal five English miles. Therefore, if a centimetre measure be carried, the distances are soon ascertained with a minimum of arithmetic.

Throughout this chapter I have taken the mathematical or map gradient and not the engineer's gradient. The latter is generally used, I understand, to measure the gradients of roads, railways, etc.

To avoid confusion when skiing, the gradient is usually named by the angle of the slope.

The gradient of slopes is shown by the contour lines, the drop between each being 30 metres or approximately 100 feet. The table on p. 92 was got out by Commander Merriman, R.N., and has proved very useful to me in setting tests as well as in judging whether slopes are comparatively safe from avalanche or not.

A slope showing eight 30-metre contour lines in one centimetre works out roughly at 27°, which is a steeper slope than most people care to take straight, running over unknown country. Anything steeper than this is apt to avalanche in certain conditions, though a 30° slope should usually be safe. (A 25° slope may be dangerous under some conditions.)

A comfortable slope is 5 contour lines in 1 centimetre, or a gradient of 17°. Taking English measurements as in Commander Merriman's scale, 16 contour lines in one inch on the map.

The beginner will probably content himself with slopes where 10 contour lines are shown in one inch, or a gradient of about 13°.

## ROUGH TABLE OF GRADIENTS.

Assuming 30 metre contours to be equal to 100 feet contours (actually this is 98.4 feet). Natural Scale 1: 50,000.

| Drop per inch | Average angle | Gradient on map of slope. |
|---|---|---|
| 100' | 1° 24' | 40.9 |
| 200' | 2° 45' | 20.8 |
| 300' | 4° 07' | 13.9 |
| 400' | 5° 29' | 10.4 |
| 500' | 6° 50' | 8.3 |
| 600' | 8° 12' | 6.9 |
| 700' | 9° 33' | 5.9 |
| 800' | 10° 52' | 5.2 |
| 900' | 12° 11' | 4.6 |
| 1,000' | 13° 30' | 4.2 |
| 1,100' | 14° 47' | 3.8 |
| 1,200' | 16° 04' | 3.5 |
| 1,300' | 17° 20' | 3.2 |
| 1,400' | 18° 34' | 3.0 |
| 1,500' | 19° 48' | 2.8 |
| 1,600' | 21° 00' | 2.6 |
| 1,700' | 22° 11' | 2.5 |
| 1,800' | 23° 22' | 2.3 |
| 1,900' | 24° 30' | 2.2 |
| 2,000' | 25° 39' | 2.1 |
| 2,100' | 26° 45' | 2.0 |
| 2,200' | 27° 50' | 1.9 |
| 2,300' | 28° 53' | 1.8 |
| 2,400' | 29° 56' | 1.7 |
| 2,500' | 30° 58' | 1.6 |

Up till now I have only been describing the official Ordnance Maps. There are several other maps which may also be useful.

The Dufour maps are good for direction and lie of country, but their scale being 1 in 100,000 they are not much help for actual running.

The local Ski Tour Map is useful to show where the usual tours go, but cannot always be trusted for gradients or cliffs and rocks. The Pontresina map, for instance, though showing an equidistance of 30 metres as in the Ordnance Maps, really has 50 metres contour lines, which might be a terrible snare to the unwary, who would confidently run towards a slope, thinking it was about 20° and find that it was nearer 35°, or an avalanche slope. In a case like this the Ordnance Map must be used for actual running, while the Ski Tour Map is used to show the line to be followed.

In some districts, such as the Bernese Oberland, the Ordnance map has been used for the local Ski tour map, and the tours shown on it in red. This is a great saving of weight and money for the runner, who then only has one map to carry.

Most Ski maps show dangerous avalanche slopes. The local Summer map published in most tourist centres in Switzerland is not much use to the Ski runner, because it shows walks which may be along slopes or down cliffs, which are perfectly safe in Summer and very dangerous in Winter.

I strongly advise all beginners who are bitten by the joy of skiing to buy, at any rate, the small local sheet of the Ordnance Map which usually only costs Frs. 1.30, or roughly 1s., and to study it carefully, noticing the contour lines on the well-known Nursery slopes, and gradually realizing the gradient represented by the different widths between them.

Let him also notice the difference between a hill and a hole on the map. This is easily recognized either by the thin blue line of a stream emerging from a lake, or by comparing the nearest heights shown on the dotted lines or some marked point. Contours are often puzzling to a beginner in map reading, but knowledge of what they represent may save a party from a weary climb back up a place they have gaily ski-ed down, thinking they could get through but finding an impossible slope or fall of rock which forced them to retrace their steps.

Before going on tour even with a Guide, it is wise to study the map with a view to knowing where an Alpine hut can be found in case of need, or where a hay châlet could offer shelter.

When once the Ski runner has begun to appreciate the fun and interest of running by a map, he will never leave it behind, and he will be able to enjoy all sorts of runs he would never know of if he were content with the sheep habit of "following tracks."

The greatest fun of skiing is in finding one's own way, and this one can never hope to do without a map.

The following scale of comparative heights in metres and feet may be of use in estimating the heights of points which the Ski runner wishes to reach:

| | |
|---|---|
| 10 metres equal | 33 feet (approximately). |
| 50 metres equal | 164 feet (approximately). |
| 100 metres equal | 328 feet (approximately). |
| 250 metres equal | 820 feet (approximately). |
| 500 metres equal | 1,640 feet (approximately). |
| 1,000 metres equal | 3,281 feet (approximately). |
| 2,000 metres equal | 6,562 feet (approximately). |
| 3,000 metres equal | 9,843 feet (approximately). |

A compass is, of course, useful when running by map, but as precipices are apt to get in the way when running straight for any given point, a compass cannot be trusted alone. In the case of fog, it is very difficult to avoid difficulties, and points on the map can only be identified by the use of an aneroid, as well as a compass. Set the aneroid at the point you start from and check your heights by this as you climb or descend, referring constantly to the map to ensure that you are running on the right line. It is wise to practise this on clear days in order to get accustomed to running by map, compass and aneroid. As the weather also affects the aneroid, it should be constantly reset at known levels.

All this may sound very confusing, and most beginners will probably prefer to take a Guide who knows his country well rather than trust to elementary map-reading knowledge in unknown country. Most runners who go on tour will find running much more interesting, however, if instead of following a Guide blindly they also watch the map or get a knowledge of what is good or bad country to run over. There are sometimes cases also when the party must necessarily divide, and an amateur may have to take the lead over unknown country.

# AVALANCHES

Much has been written on this subject. Mr. Arnold Lunn, in "The Alps," tells some extraordinary stories about these monsters of the mountains. My father, John Addington Symonds, in "Our Life in the Swiss Highlands," also describes them.

There was a very interesting article by Monsieur F. Krahnstoever in the "Swiss Ski Club Year-Book for 1923" on the subject of avalanches in relation to Skiing. They are an everlasting nightmare to Ski runners in high places, and beginners should at once take care to learn all they can of snow-craft in order, in so far as possible, to realize what is safe and what is dangerous.

The steepness of slopes and the condition of snow, as well as the direction of wind, are all factors affecting avalanches.

Any slope whose gradient is more than 15° may be dangerous under certain conditions, but it may be generally accepted that most long slopes under 25° are comparatively safe so long as they have not much steeper slopes immediately above or below them.

New snow is always apt to slip before it has had time to settle down. Snow blown by wind into a cornice or overhanging lip at the top of a slope or on a cliff may topple down and start an avalanche.

Wet snow, after rain, or a warm Föhn wind, becomes heavy and begins to slide.

A very dangerous condition is new soft snow lying on a slope covered with old hard snow.

Trees or rocks sticking up through the snow make such slopes safer, as they tend to prevent the snow from beginning to slip. This is why the Forestry Laws of Switzerland are so strict. In some districts the owner of a forest may not cut a tree unless it has been approved by the Government forester. This is to ensure that the forests are maintained as a protection for the villages in the valleys below.

Beginners should never go on a tour without first ascertaining that the route they propose to follow is a safe one. And if there is the slightest doubt, owing to weather conditions, they should put it off for a day or two. Some runs are perfectly safe when the snow has settled and a sharp frost has bound it, but they may become dangerous again when a thaw sets in, a Föhn wind is blowing, or rain has fallen.

The Ski runner himself may start an avalanche on a slope where the snow would lie safely if he did not pass along it. The cutting of his track, breaking the continuity of the snow, may set it going either above or below him and he will be carried away with it.

Wherever there seems to be the slightest risk of avalanche the party should separate and proceed in single file at about 20-yard intervals. Then if a runner is carried away, the others will be able to go to his assistance. In some cases, however, even this is not sufficient protection as the whole slope may go at once. In old days before the railways had tunnelled through the passes we were driving over the Fluela above Davos on our way to Italy in March. We were in the post consisting of some 20 one-horse sledges and had just left the Hospiz when we met the up-coming post, also consisting of a number of one-horse sledges. It took some time to pass, as the track was narrow and the horses floundered in the deep snow when passing each other. After we had got by and were continuing on our way down to Süs, we turned along an outstanding buttress of cliff and saw that some two miles of steep slope ahead had avalanched. The whole surface of the snow had slipped to the bottom of the valley and if either of the diligences had been on this slope when it happened, horses, sledges and all would have been carried away.

This experience fixed avalanche danger very firmly in my mind, and having also seen several large avalanches falling, as well as the immense amount of damage done to forests and châlets by these insuperable monsters, I have never wished to risk getting into a large one myself.

Even a small avalanche is very overwhelming and a beginner who has felt its effects soon realizes what it may mean. Choose a *very* short steep slope on a day when the snow is slipping and try to get it going. Once it moves and entangles your legs and Skis, you will feel the extraordinary helplessness which results. This was one of our games when I was a child. Without Skis it is possible to float on top of a baby avalanche and to enjoy it, but with Skis on, the feet soon become entangled and helplessness results.

The first thing to do when an avalanche starts and no escape is possible is to get the Ski bindings undone and the feet free. Then "swim" with arms and legs and try to keep on top. If buried, keep one arm over nose and mouth so as to keep air space and push the other arm up, pointing the Ski stick through to the open so that it may show your whereabouts. This is easy to describe, but probably not so easy to carry out if the occasion arises.

One of the first books on Ski-running advises people to carry some 60 metres of red tape and to let this trail behind them when crossing dangerous ground. Then, if overwhelmed by an avalanche, the red thread can be picked up by the search party and the victim may quickly be dug out. I have never met anyone who has carried out this suggestion and do not want the extra weight of red tape in my Rucksack, but it makes one think and realize how much other experienced runners have thought also.

The following precautions would seem to me to be better:

Never ski along, or above, or below a dangerous-looking slope under doubtful conditions.

Never go for a tour without making sure beforehand that the route you propose to follow is a safe one.

Always carry out any instructions your Guide or the experienced leader of your party may give. If you have any sudden doubt about the safety of the slope you are on, make quickly for the nearest rocks sticking up.

If there are trees near get among them as quickly and quietly as you can.

If the snow begins to slip and you see no chance of skiing quickly away from the dangerous place, get your Skis off. This is where toe bindings may be safer than heel bindings as they come off quicker.

Never follow a track across a slope, about which you are doubtful, thinking hopefully that the runner who cut it knew more than yourself.

Never cut a track across a dangerous place at your own risk if there is the slightest chance of misleading another runner into danger later.

Remember that though you yourself may be on a safe slope, the slope above or below you may be so steep that the snow may slip off by itself and your slope may be involved. This applies equally to running along the bottom of a valley. The slopes on either side may be dangerous, and if the snow slips you will be buried.

There are so many perfectly safe runs that it is folly to risk being killed by an avalanche, when it can easily be avoided by a little forethought and common sense.

Even if you do not mind the risk yourself, think not only of your people waiting below, but also of the people who have to come and look for your body. There have been several cases where the search party have been overwhelmed by a second avalanche while digging for people carried away by the first.

January and March are probably the most dangerous months from the avalanche point of view. In January the fresh snow is apt to slide before it has settled. A few days after a new snowfall, most of the avalanches will have come down and the ordinary runs will be safe again, but every snowfall entails the same risk. There are some slopes where the snow will never stay in February, but unless a Föhn wind or rain make the snow heavy, most slopes are pretty safe below a gradient of 25°.

In March when the thaw begins more avalanches will fall. These usually come down well-known tracks and can easily be avoided for this reason.

This chapter may appear to be somewhat intimidating, but it is better to be safe than sorry. Very few experienced Ski runners get into avalanches and if ordinary precautions are taken and the advice of experts followed beginners need have no fear.

The Skiing maps usually show the more dangerous places, but every runner should keep his own eyes open and learn all he can of snow-craft in order to be able to explore new country as he becomes proficient.

# ACCIDENTS

Some people will think that I lay too much stress on the dangers of skiing. Considering the thousands of people who ski every Winter and the extraordinarily small number of accidents, I admit that I have exaggerated the dangers. But I do so quite deliberately because it is only by realizing risks that they can be avoided, and my experience proves to me that the average town-bred man and woman, boy and girl have very little appreciation of life lived up against Nature. They set out so lightheartedly and often so fool-hardily on an expedition, without telling anyone where they propose to go, or when they expect to be home, and without having provided themselves with the extra equipment which may prove to be very necessary before the day is finished.

While writing this book I have constantly had in mind Skiing centres above 5,000 feet, whence tours are made among the glaciers and at high levels where the cold may be a danger during the months of January and February. Much of what I have said of the necessity of carrying spare clothing in good quantity does not apply so much to places below 5,000 feet unless high tours are undertaken. But wherever people ski there is a possibility of accidents due to falls, and though these are seldom serious, they need attention.

When someone is really lamed by knee or ankle, Skiing becomes very difficult, except to the expert, who can ski mainly on one foot, and walking through the deep snow, sinking at every step, is an agony, so that some form of stretcher becomes necessary.

Two or, better still, four Skis tied together, side by side, form an excellent sledge, which will travel straight downhill every easily. It practically refuses to traverse a slope so that the case has to be slipped straight down to the bottom of the slope and along the valley or level below.

Skis usually have holes through the flat part of the tip in front. A piece of strong wire should be threaded through these, care being taken that the Skis lie parallel their whole length and that the tips are not drawn together too much. A stick must be tied to the wire and the Ski tips to keep them in position and to take the pull when the sledge is drawn along. If there are trees about, a branch can be cut to serve this purpose. If not, a Ski stick must be cut in half and used. It should not project beyond the Skis on either side, or it will catch in the snow.

The other half of the Ski stick or another branch must be tied across the Skis, by the toe irons, to keep the Skis parallel there also, and to give solidity to the sledge. People sometimes tie a strap or string round the Skis, including their running surfaces, forgetting that this will soon cut through with the friction of the snow.

To finish the sledge, put some fir branches on it, the bushy part of which will make it more comfortable to lie on. The thick wood of the branch part should point towards the front of the Skis and be fixed there. If branches are not available, Rucksacks can be used for the injured person to lie on. He will probably be more comfortable going downhill if he can be laid head-first downwards on the sledge.

To draw the sledge along, join a lap thong or sealskin or rope or puttee to the outer Ski tips, and also to the ends of the stick across them. In order to prevent this from pulling these Skis forward too much it is well to tie a string to the inner Ski tips also and join them to the pulling rope.

Another rope or thong should be attached to the stick and centre toe irons, so that this can be held from behind to prevent the sledge travelling too fast downhill. Experienced runners will be able to travel on Skis while getting this sledge down, but beginners will do well to wade on foot, especially the rear man, who has to control the speed. Neither the pulling nor control rope should be attached to the body of the person holding it because a sudden jerk may pull him over and the sledge be stopped suddenly with a jar to the person hurt.

Most club huts are provided with excellent ambulance sledges, which may be used, and which should be conscientiously returned to the Rettungschef of the locality.

There is a Rettungschef in every mountainous district whose duty it is to help with accidents when these are reported to him. He arranges to send out Guides and porters with an ambulance sledge to the assistance of any party in trouble. If, therefore, your accident be a serious one, and you are far from home, the wisest plan may be to send one or two of the best runners down to the nearest village for help, while the remainder stay with the injured person. For this reason it is always unwise to go out with fewer than three in a party. Five or six are a better number on a long day's run.

Remember the people waiting at home, and when you have made arrangements for help to go to your party ring up your friends and tell them what has happened and what you have arranged. Having often seen the anxiety of relations and friends when their party comes home late, I know how important this is. Even if you are only delayed for some small reason such as a train being late, it is kind to ring up, and this is easily done, as there are telephones in almost every village.

While on this subject I would again like to urge that before going off on an expedition of any length the Concierge and someone should be told in writing the destination, the route, and the hour anticipated for return. Then, if the party does not turn up and no news comes through, a search party can be sent out with some hope of finding them within a reasonable time. Time is very important in January and February, when the weather is cold, as people can be badly frost-bitten if benighted.

Search parties are expensive luxuries, as it is risky work for the Guides, who deserve to be well paid for it. I have only once followed a Rettungschef with his five assistants and their ambulance sledge, and shall never forget the pace at which their lantern went ahead of us, dancing like a will-of-the-wisp. A runner had come home at 5 p.m. with news that one of the party had hurt his knee some four miles from home. This runner had already wisely rung up the Rettungschef from the first house he came to, and a party of Guides was being collected. I decided to go out with some friends in case the accident was a serious one and we could bring the remainder of the party home, and so save the Guides that duty. They were all beginners who were benighted.

We followed the lantern and saw it stop and knew the Guides had reached the people in trouble. When we caught up they already had the patient looking like a mummy, rolled up in blankets in a canvas bag on the sledge. I could hear him choking over the brandy which was being poured down his throat. He had only hurt his knee, but his friends, who were all real novices, had had a wearing time getting him down.

The way in which the Guides handled the job filled me with admiration and confidence. When they found we were ready to herd the party home, they shot off with their sledge and the lantern soon became a speck of light in the distance again.

I also had a lantern that night, and found it delightful to ski by, but doubt whether anyone else profited much by its light except as a guide to direction.

When a person is hurt and helpless at a high level, in winter, cold is the most immediate danger, and all spare clothing should be piled on him, and his limbs should be rubbed to prevent frost-bite. When he cannot be moved, a fire might well be lit if below tree level where wood is available, because, though the lighting of fires is forbidden in the Swiss forests, a breach of the law would surely be overlooked in case of danger to life. The heat of the fire would help to keep the patient warm, while its light would act as a beacon to the search party.

The following is the code of signals in use among the Alps:

## THE ALPINE SIGNAL OF DISTRESS—

(a) By Day.—The waving of anything (a flag or stick with an article of clothing attached) six times in a minute, repeated after an interval of one minute without signals.

(b) By Night.—A light flashed six times a minute, repeated after an interval of one minute without signals.

(c) By Sound.—Six sharp calls, or whistles, in the minute, repeated after an interval of one minute without signals.

## THE ANSWERING CALL—

(d) Anything waved, a light flashed, a sharp call, or whistle three times in the minute, repeated after an interval of one minute without signals.

If a Ski runner does not remember the exact signal any regular signal repeated a definite number of times in a minute, with a minute's interval, should prove sufficient. Similarly, if you hear a signal repeated at short regular intervals, you should always suspect a call for help.

An ordinary whistle is hardly loud enough for the sound to carry any distance and a siren might be better. Newspaper could be used for a flare if the party does not possess a lantern or electric torch, but it would not last long.

Finally, may I suggest that everyone who takes up Skiing seriously, and who carries gear to be used in emergency, should be proficient in the use of such gear and not wait till it is needed to find out how to fit it.

To experiment in making an ambulance sledge while an injured person lies beside you and when your fingers are cold and people are buzzing round you with suggestions, which may or may not be better than your own ideas, is a bad plan. It is wiser to have made the experiment at home and to have got someone to drag you down a hill on the result, and then you will know something about it. A new game for the Nursery slopes, and what fun for the spectators who already think all Skiers mad!

I would like to add at the end of this chapter on accidents that during the many years I have enjoyed Skiing, and with the hundreds of beginners I have helped, I have never met with a single really serious accident.

One or two knees and ankles twisted and now and then a cut or severe bruise have been among the worst cases I have come across.

# THE ATTRACTIONS OF SKIING

Though some runners are content merely to enjoy the actual practice of skiing with all the difficulties to be overcome and the various turns to be perfected, the greater proportion probably ski mainly on account of the exhilaration obtained, the freedom enjoyed, and the wonderful beauty of the places reached.

The amazing thing is that Skis were not used sooner among the Alps. They have already in less than thirty years entirely altered the life of the young people in far-away villages, who used to be practically shut up during the winter months, but who can now ski from one place to another on Sundays and holidays, enjoying the companionship of their friends and widening their outlook by mixing with strangers. This will probably have a very good effect on the population of the High Alps, who will be less inclined to leave their homes in order to get away from the monotony of the long winters. So much is this appreciated that Skiing is now part of the school curriculum in some districts, often taking the place of gymnastics during the winter.

It is amusing to watch the classes of children out on the Nursery slopes with their teachers. While we foreign women Ski-runners are provided with elaborate costumes, including breeches or trousers, the little Swiss girls ski in frocks and cotton pinafores without cap or hat, and often without gloves. Led by their teacher they wearily climb up the slopes, and then comes the mad career home to the midday meal. Twenty or thirty little girls all dashing down together practising turns as they go, or making as straight down as they dare in their effort to outpace their rivals.

The boys carry the sport still further and most local Ski-jumping competitions start with a demonstration by the boys, who often do not look more than 10 or 12 years old, and who go over the big jump as straight as their elders and usually a good deal more gaily, as they have not begun to appreciate the dangers. The smaller boys line the sides of the jump and pour out at the word of the judge on to the steep landing-slope like a lot of little goblins, jumping on their Skis horizontally to flatten away any track or hole made by a jumper who has failed to jump perfectly. Little chaps of seven or eight run through the woods on these occasions, swanking their turns through the trees and putting most grown-up runners to shame by their nimbleness. At Pontresina one winter I was much amused by one of these small children wearing a British third-class test badge which he must have picked up. I asked him where he got it, but he hurried away for fear I would claim it, and his Christianias through the big trees made me very envious.

Many of the children ski to school and back, getting endless practice all through the winter months.

May I here appeal to British runners who may have old Skis, even broken ones to throw away, to offer them to the local branch of the Swiss Ski Club as there is an organization which mends them or cuts them down for lending or giving to the school children, who are too poor to provide themselves with Skis.

When the beginner has learnt the elements of straight running and turns and begins to go off among the mountains the real interest of skiing is begun, with the slow climb up in single file, first of all through woods and then out on to the open slopes. This is usually a silent game as breath is needed for the climb, and it is dull work keeping up a conversation with the back ahead. Sometimes, as one inadvertently steps on the Skis ahead, a gruff word is flung back and the trespasser is wise who stops, pretending to attend to his binding, or to look at the view—the view is usually worth looking at, too, as there is usually something to see. If it is not a distant view of the Great Alps or of the valley below, it is of trees or rocks, which, if examined carefully, usually show some sign of life. I remember being snubbed by an ardent Ski-er because I ventured to ask "What are those black birds?" "Who wants to know about birds when he is skiing?" was the answer. I did want to know, and I found out that they were Alpine choughs and I still want to know when I see the inhabitants of the mountains or their tracks.

Most of the wild animals use old Ski tracks as highways now, even finding it worth while to follow the zigzag of an uphill traverse. Foxes, hares and roe deer all use them, the roe deers' feet showing so much tinier than the chamois, who leaves a deep rough track as they usually run in each other's footsteps. The hare's track when running is two holes abreast and then two single ones. The fox runs rather like a dog. The squirrel hops two feet at a time, often leaving a slight ruffle on the snow as he swishes his tail. Among the cembra trees in the Engadine the snow may be sprinkled with the nuts out of the cones. They are delicious eating, being very like the Italian stone pine nut, or pinelli, and they attract the squirrels as much as they do the nutcracker bird.

Martens and pole cats leave distinct footmarks. Weasels, also, and these are easily recognized as they usually start from a hole under a bush or a rock. One day when a party of us were silently traversing a slope above Mürren a tiny brown ball came rolling down, which, when picked up, proved to be the warm dead body of a mouse. Looking up we saw a weasel peering out of his hole anxious as to the fate of his dinner. A mouse's track also usually starts from a tiny hole and the two feet go abreast, while the tail leaves a line all the way.

We nearly always see chamois and roe deer when skiing in the woods at Pontresina as it is a protected area and they are not shot and therefore become very tame. The chamois are driven down into the woods in search of the lichen which hangs like a beard from the branches of the cembra trees. On Muottas Celerina this winter we saw four chamois below us in the wood. Without a word our guide, Caspar Gras, dashed down the slope after them and very nearly caught one round the neck, as they were surprised, and knowing there was a precipice beyond the scrub below them, they could not make up their minds which way to go.

The roe deer scrape away the snow below the trees in search of alpenrose or bear berry leaves or dry blades of grass. They suffer more than the chamois after a heavy snowfall because they are not so strong and cannot scamper through it. At the beginning of this season, Klosters had a snowfall of some two metres and the roe deer were driven down to the villages where the peasants fed them in stables till the weather improved. Four were caught on the railway, having got on to the line at a crossing and being unable to spring out over the high banks of snow.

Ibex are being let loose in order to re-establish them where they were exterminated a few years ago. They can usually be seen through the telescope at Bernina Hauser above Pontresina, and also opposite Mürren. The ibex, or steinbock, is used as the Coat of Arms of the Canton of Graubünden, and is familiar to Ski runners as the badge of the local Ski Club of Zuoz in the Engadine.

After some controversy eagles are being encouraged to increase, having been almost exterminated. We saw a beauty sailing over the Muottas Muraigl Valley one day. There is even talk of trying to get bear back, but the peasants obstruct this as they were so destructive to sheep. As a child at Davos I saw three bears brought in dead by hunters, and remember with pride, mixed with disgust, tasting a bear's paw. A peasant told me of how as a boy he looked after the village sheep near the Silvretta Glacier, and of a bear who used to come and kill a sheep and then bury it in the ice for future eating.

Ski runners shudder at the idea of meeting a bear while on a run, but they need not worry as the bears roll up and sleep through the winter so that unless the Ski-er took an unusually heavy fall into the bear's hole, he would be safe enough on the surface. Besides which it is said that a bear cannot traverse down a slope, so that the Ski-er could easily get away unless the bear rolled to the bottom, and then ran along and waited for him. As there are no bears in Switzerland now, perhaps it is waste of time to start a controversy about the best turn with which to circumvent a bear. Cows are much more dangerous. I was pursued down the village street at Pontresina by a playful cow, who had been taken to the pump to drink. She put down her head and stuck up her tail and I wasted no time in pushing away from her.

Another animal which hibernates through the winter is the marmot, and I often think of them sound asleep under the snow as I pass along the slopes of some high valley. They are said to have breathing holes, but I have never seen them, unless this was the explanation of some holes which puzzled me on the Schiltgrat above Mürren. I was traversing uphill a long way ahead of my party and noticed some isolated holes in the snow, very like Ski stick holes, but with no Ski tracks near. As I passed a grey hen flew out of one of the holes, and, looking back, I saw several black cocks and grey hens flying away. It is more likely that they had made their own holes to shelter in rather than that these were marmot holes.

Ptarmigan often greet one on the higher ridges and sometimes a capercailzie will get up with a noise which is very apt to upset one.

The choughs are persistent followers of a Skiing party, flying over one's head and chirruping for lunch. When at last we stop and take our nosebags out of our Rucksacks, they perch on a cliff near and wait till we move on, when they immediately fly down to see what we have left for them. I have seen a paper lunch-bag, which they were unable to tear, absolutely surrounded by a circle of their footmarks, some eight feet in diameter. How they must have worried it and each other in their endeavour to get at the contents.

At Mürren a pair of ravens also accompany the Ski-ers. They take their perch high up and watch the many luncheon parties, croaking now and then to remind us of their wish to share our slices of beef and sausage. These "packed lunches" are usually so plentiful that the choughs and the ravens get a goodly feed. The tidy Ski-er who buries all his paper and orange peel and other debris will often find next day that the whole thing has been dug up by a fox.

At many of the Alpine huts, the snow-finch has adopted the habits of the sparrow and is often so tame that he will almost take crumbs from one's hand.

Another bird I love among the Alps is the dipper or water ouzel. Skiing along the snow banks of the rivers, I have often watched him hop down into the water and run along the bottom picking up whatever his food is among the pebbles.

Surely most Ski runners can spare time to watch all these little people, whose rights to the snow fields are even greater than their own.

Very little vegetation shows in winter, but it is wonderful what a lot one can find if one looks carefully and it certainly makes Skiing more interesting to me if I can recognize the trees, plants and seeds.

A very fair estimate can be made of the different heights by noticing what grows.

Corn stops at 2,000 to 3,000 feet, though a little rye may be grown up to 5,000 feet in sunny places. Fruit trees and beech trees stop at about 4,000 feet. There is one beech tree above Davos about 5,500 feet above the sea, but it has never succeeded in topping the huge boulder which shelters it from the North. The silver fir is healthy at 4,000 feet, but is seldom found much above that level, while the spruce or fir goes up to 7,000 feet and does best there. Larches seem to thrive best at about 5,000-6,000 feet, but may be seen almost as high as the top of the Bernina Pass on the south side facing Italy. The cembra pine, like a great cedar, is the finest tree in the Alps and does best at 6,000 feet to 7,000 feet. It is also called the Arolla pine, because of the forests near that place. In the Upper Engadine almost all the forests are of cembra and there is one splendid old tree known as the "Giant Tree" near upper tree level on Muottas Celerina. Another group of veterans grows just below the Little Scheidegg on the Grindelwald side. Many of these trees are said to be 600 or 700 years old and their wood is much used for panelling in Graubünden. It is recognized by the big dark knots. The panels are usually formed of boards reversed so that the knots form a symmetrical pattern. Larch is also used and is very red, while sycamore goes to the making of tables and chairs in the Bündner Stübli. Good examples of the modern use of these woods may be seen in the hotels, Vereina and Silvretta, at Klosters, while the museum at Zurich contains beautiful old panelled rooms from different districts.

Creeping down steep avalanche slopes above 5,000 feet we find *Pinus montana*, whose long branches form a tangle in which to catch one's Ski tips. Below 5,000 feet this pine will sometimes grow almost upright but never attains much height. Alder may also be a trap for Skis on an avalanche slope where it creeps downhill and provides a very slippery surface for the snow. I remember shooting down such a slope about 100 feet when the snow slipped with me in a safe place.

Along the rivers the alder grows into quite a fine tree, and if its catkins be picked at Christmas and are brought into the warm house, they soon blossom out and spread their green pollen over everything. Rather a nice way of bringing a reminder of Spring into one's Winter holiday.

Birch and mountain ash grow happily up to 6,000 feet on sheltered slopes but after 6,000 feet there are no deciduous trees, except the tiny creeping willows buried deep under the snow.

Juniper is the most ubiquitous shrub to be found, it seems to me. You get its various types at sea level in Italy and on the top of mountains up to 8,000 feet when it pokes up through the snow beside the Alpine Rose or *Rhododendron ferrugineum*.

On the top of ridges when the snow is blown away, all sorts of treasures may be recognized. The creeping azalea with its wee evergreen leaves, which no one, thinking of the garden azaleas at home, would recognize as belonging to the same family. Little primulas and saxifrages sheltering in cracks in the rocks, with nothing but bunches of brown leaves to show them up. *Polygula Chamaebuxis* or Bastard Box almost always in flower on a sunny patch even in midwinter. On the lower slopes, gentians or anemone plants with their buds waiting to open when the soft wind or rain of Spring calls to them. *Erica carnea* with its whitish buds waiting for Spring to colour them, one of the earliest of the flowers. Or the seeds of *Gentiana lutea* or *asclepedia* or *purpurea* and of Aconite or Monkshood on their strong stems standing high above the snow.

One winter when at 4,000 feet we had no snow at Christmas, we went flower hunting instead of skiing, and found thirty different sorts of flowers out. But this was exceptional and by no means satisfying to the Ski runner, who has come out for the sport he loves and not on botany intent.

Later, when the snow begins to melt on South slopes in March, the mass of purple and white crocuses open to the sun; nothing in the whole world can equal the mass of these crocuses. They push up as the miracle of Spring, impatiently thrusting through the snow, melting holes for themselves. The soldanellas do the same, but not till late in March, and with them come gentians and the whole glory of the Alpine Spring has begun. By this time the Ski-er has to oil and put away his Skis or climb to the glaciers and higher snow fields. A wonderful experience alternating between Spring and Winter as he changes his levels.

# SUMMER SKIING

The only experience of Summer skiing which I have had is on the Jungfrau Joch, about 11,900 feet above the sea.

The Berner Oberland and Jungfrau Railways carry one up from Interlaken to the Joch where there is an excellent new hotel, offering every possible comfort.

Good Skiing can be had on the glaciers and I am surprised that more people do not come out for practice during the Summer.

The two great draw-backs to this Skiing are, firstly, the expense and, secondly, the difficulty of breathing. The expense is unavoidable because the carriage of building materials, food, etc. to such a height must necessarily entail high prices. Glacier skiing, except on the snow-field near the Joch, also usually necessitates the employment of Guides. But these snow-fields are so extensive and so safe that a week could be spent in practising without a Guide.

After the first night on the Joch the feeling of breathlessness is reduced, and so long as all climbing is done slowly no bad effects need be expected by people in good health and condition. The Jungfrau Joch can be reached from London in twenty-six hours, and keen runners could enjoy a week or a fortnight of amusing Skiing on snow which lends itself particularly well to the practice of all turns.

The Jungfrau Joch branch of the Swiss Ski Club holds an annual meet on the Joch in the month of July, which is well attended by Runners and Jumpers from all parts of Switzerland.

First-Class Guides and Ski Instructors can be found at the Joch.

People who would prefer not to sleep at so great a height could stay at the Scheidegg or Eiger Gletscher, at both of which places hotels exist.

In view of the shortness of Winter holidays, it seems a pity that more enthusiasts do not profit by the chance of practising which the Jungfrau Joch Railway offers in Summer time. I have twice spent two days up there and have enjoyed them immensely. The snow was very different to anything I ever met in Winter, but also very easy and filled me with confidence. In July and August the crevasses show clearly and need not inspire anxiety in anyone, except after a new fall of snow, which may hide the smaller ones temporarily again.

There must be several square miles of perfectly safe Skiing on the glaciers behind the Joch, which provide Nursery slopes just as good as anything found in Winter. The gradients vary, but it is easy to find stretches of 10° to 30° unbroken by crevasses.

Anyone coming out to ski on the glaciers in Summer time should bring with them their own Skis or arrange to hire these at some Winter

Sports centre in the valleys. They should also be provided with all the skiing equipment they may need. A few pairs of Skis are kept for hiring purposes on the Jungfrau Joch, but they are not very good ones and it would be better not to depend on them.

# REGULATIONS OF THE BRITISH SKI TESTS

## AS APPROVED BY THE FEDERAL COUNCIL
## OF BRITISH SKI CLUBS. 1923.

GENERAL REGULATIONS.

1. The British Standard Ski Tests have been drawn up by the Federal Council of British Ski Clubs, hereinafter referred to as "The Council." *The Council represents the following clubs, which are named in the order of their foundation: The Davos Ski Club, the Ski Club of Great Britain, the Alpine Ski Club, the British Ski Association, and the Ladies' Ski Club.*

2. The British Standard Ski Tests are of two kinds: Cross Country Skiing Tests and Jumping Tests. There are three Tests of each kind, a First Class Test, a Second Class Test, and a Third Class Test.

3. The Tests are open to all ski-runners without payment, but successful candidates will only receive a certificate and badge if they are members or prospective members of one of the Clubs represented on the Council. A candidate who has been proposed and seconded for a constituent Club, and who has paid a year's subscription, and whose election is pending, will be deemed a prospective member for the purpose of this rule. The following sums will be payable for the badges. These sums may be paid through the members' Clubs or direct to the Hon. Secretary of the Council.

First Class Badge 35s. Second Class Badge 3s. Third Class Badge 2s.

4. In Switzerland francs will be accepted instead of shillings in payment of badges.

5. Certificates and badges will be awarded to any person who has passed the Cross Country Skiing Tests: First Class, a gold badge; Second Class, a silver badge; Third Class, a bronze badge. Certificates will be issued to those who have passed the corresponding Jumping Tests, and these certificates will entitle the holder to receive a Jumping badge when the Council authorizes the issue of new badges.

6. Application for the badges, accompanied by a certificate signed by two judges, shall be made either to the local representative of the Club or to the Hon. Secretary of the Council, K.R. Swan, Esq., 1 Essex Court, Temple, within three months of the passing of the Test.

7. Certificate holders will alone be recognized as having passed the tests. *No certificate will be recognized as valid unless issued to a member*

*of one of the constituent clubs of the Council.* A list of those certified as having passed any of the tests will be issued periodically by the Council.

8. *Judges.*—No candidate can be judged for any test nor for any part of a test unless two qualified Judges are present. No candidate can be passed for any part of a test except by being judged formally and knowing that he is being judged.

9. The Judges are appointed by the Council; the appointment is for the season only. Judges and Emergency Judges must be of British nationality.

10. The Council also appoints an emergency committee, any one of whom shall have the power to appoint temporary judges for the season only, to act with a Judge elected by the Council. Such temporary judges shall only be qualified to judge such tests as they have themselves passed. The appointment of an Emergency Judge will not be recognized by the Council unless the appointment is notified to the Secretary of the Council.

## CROSS COUNTRY SKIING TESTS.

GENERAL INSTRUCTIONS TO JUDGES.

The following definitions may be taken as applying to the three tests:

*Stemming Turns.*—For the purpose of these Tests, Judges must insist that candidates shall adopt that type of stemming turn known as the "lifted stemming turn," that is to say, the stemming turn which is finished by lifting round the inside ski.

*Telemarks.*—In the Telemark the back ski should drop behind, and the bend of the back ski should not be ahead of the ankle of the leading foot and should not be allowed to come forward till the turn is completed. Candidates who start the turn with a mixture of ordinary stemming should not be passed.

*Christianias.*—The Christiania may be done either by separating the points of the ski and completed by bringing them parallel—the so-called "open Christiania"; *or* by keeping the ski parallel throughout and jerking them round, the "jerked Christiania"; *or* by a very slight stem, the ski being immediately brought parallel after the turn has started, the so-called "Closed or Stem Christiania."

In every case the essence of the Christiania is that the swing should be rapid, and that the preliminary stemming or diverging of the skis should be as slight as possible.

A turn started by pronounced stemming and completed as a Christiania should not be passed.

*Continuous Turns* are sometimes known as "downhill turns." They are used to connect one tack with another, and differ from stop or uphill turns in that the turn is made away from the hill instead of up towards the hill. Candidates must not stop between two continuous turns.

*Hard Snow.*—For the purpose of these tests, any well-beaten down practice slope from which all traces of soft snow have disappeared may be considered as hard snow. Hard crust superficially softened by the sun cannot be considered as hard snow.

*Soft Snow.*—For the purpose of these tests, a deep layer of powder snow resting on hard crust, or hard crust superficially softened by the sun, but not breakable, may be considered as soft snow.

*Form.*—The Judges must consider the "form" of the runner, as well as his speed and steadiness. The distinguishing marks of good "form" are an easy balance without dependence on the sticks (see below), an erect position, except on steep slopes, and a narrow single spoor in soft snow.

*Use of the Sticks.*—Candidates should carry sticks throughout these tests, but the sticks should not be used to reduce speed nor to help out a turn. On the other hand, a candidate may be allowed a prod with a single stick at the end of a turn provided that he is carrying a stick in each hand, or in the event of the candidate using a single stick that this stick is only held in one of his hands. *He must not put both his sticks together, nor hold a single stick in his two hands, during any of these tests, unless expressly directed to do so by the Judge.*

## THE THIRD CLASS TEST (CROSS COUNTRY).

The Third Class Test consists of three parts, which may be passed on different days, and before different Judges.

Part (a).—*The ascent of 1,500 feet in not more than 1 hour 30 minutes, and the descent of the same distance within a time which shall be decided by the Judges. This time shall not be less than 7 minutes, nor more than 20 minutes, and shall not exceed 12 minutes unless sanctioned by a Second Class Judge or member of the Emergency Committee who is present and judging.*

Part (b).—*Four continuous Lifted Stemming turns on a slope of hard snow or hard snow covered by a shallow layer of soft snow. The angle of the slope to be between 15-20 degrees.*

Part (c).—*Four continuous Telemarks in soft snow on a slope of similar gradient.*

INSTRUCTIONS TO JUDGES.

1. The course selected for Part (a) should include at least 200 feet of moderately difficult ground. Courses such as the Lauberhorn at Wengen, which is an unbroken descent of 1,500 feet that a good runner could take straight, should not be chosen. No part of the course should be along a road.

2. Throughout the Test candidates must carry rucksacks, which should weigh about six lbs. for men, and three lbs. for ladies. The ski must not be removed during the test, except to clean or repair them.

3. The Judges should, if possible, appoint two time-keepers. During the descent not more than six candidates must be judged in one batch.

4. Not more than three attempts at Part (b), and not more than three attempts at Part (c) are allowed on the same day.

5. The attention of the Judges is directed to the General Instructions. The gradient on which Third Class candidates are expected to do their turns is gentle, as the intention is to secure that candidates should master the proper methods, so as to be able later to make real use of the turns on steep slopes. Judges are therefore urged to insist that the stemming turns and Telemarks are done correctly and in good style. Each turn should be short, well defined, and not a mere change of direction.

## QUALIFYING TEST FOR THE SECOND CLASS (CROSS COUNTRY).

No Candidate may enter for Parts (a), (b) and (c) of the Second Class Test until he has passed the Qualifying Test, and no Candidate may enter for the Qualifying Test until he has passed the Third Class Test.

The Qualifying Test consists of three parts, which may be passed on different days and before different judges, but which must all be passed in the same season.

Part (a).—*Four continuous Lifted Stemming turns on a slope of hard snow at an angle of 25-30 degrees.*

Part (b).—*Four continuous Telemark turns on a slope of soft snow at an angle of 25-30 degrees.*

Part (c).—*Christiania swings to a standstill (right and left) from a direct descent at a fair speed.*

INSTRUCTIONS TO JUDGES.

1. Not more than three attempts at any one part should be allowed on the same day.

2. The Christianias should be done on the level or on a gentle slope after a descent from a steep slope, as a stop Christiania is more difficult on the level than on the slope.

3. The Judges must require a considerably higher standard of steadiness and certainty than in the Third Class Test. The object of the Third Class Test is to ensure that candidates learn the correct methods of making the turns. The object of the Second Class Test is to ensure that candidates can make practical use of these turns on moderately steep slopes.

## THE SECOND CLASS TEST (CROSS COUNTRY).

The Second Class Test consists of three parts, which must all be passed in the same season, and should, if possible, be judged by the same Judges.

> Part (a).—*A descent of not less than 2,500 feet, mainly on soft snow. The course selected should provide opportunities for straight running on reasonably steep slopes.*
> Part (b).—*A descent of not less than 1,000 feet on hard snow, such as unbreakable crust or snow which has been thoroughly beaten down.*
> Part (c).—*A descent of at least 500 feet of woodrunning, dense enough to prevent straight running, but not too dense to prevent continuous turns.*

1. A Second Class runner may be defined as a runner who can run at a good speed on hard or soft snow of unvarying quality, and who is, above all, thoroughly steady on his turns. A runner who runs recklessly without judgment, and who shows little power of selecting a safe line, should not be passed even if he takes slopes straight at the expense of frequent falls. *The Second Class Test is, in the main, a test of steady controlled skiing at a good, but not at a racing speed.*

2. Candidates must not use their sticks to control speed nor to help out a turn except under very exceptional circumstances and with the express permission of the Judges. The Judges must, however, satisfy themselves that the Candidates understand the use of the stick, and could, in emergencies, where speed is vital, increase their speed and steadiness on difficult snow by the use of the stick.

# QUALIFYING TEST FOR THE FIRST CLASS (CROSS COUNTRY).

No candidate may enter for Parts (a), (b) and (c) of the First Class Test until he has passed the Qualifying Test that entitles him to be judged for the First Class Test, and no candidate may enter for this Qualifying Test until he has passed the Second Class Test.

The Qualifying Test consists of five parts, which may be judged on different days and before different Judges, but which must all be passed in the same season.

Part (a).—*Four continuous lifted Stemming turns on a slope of hard snow at an angle of not less than 30 degrees.*

Part (b).—*Four continuous Telemark turns on a slope of soft snow at an angle of not less than 30.*

Part (c).—*Four consecutive jump-turns to connect downhill tacks on a slope of breakable crust at an angle of about 30 degrees.*

Part (d).—*Christiania swings to a standstill (right and left) from a direct descent at a very high speed.*

Part (e).—*Four continuous Christiania (see General Instructions) on a slope of about 20 degrees.*

INSTRUCTIONS TO JUDGES.

1. The turns must be done round sticks or flags placed by the Judges.

2. Not more than three attempts at any one part are allowed on the same day.

3. Soft breakable crust will usually be found on slopes with a southerly exposure just after the sun has struck them or just before the sun leaves them.

# FIRST CLASS TEST (CROSS COUNTRY SKIING).

The First Class Test consists of three parts, which must all be passed in the same season and should, if possible, be passed by the same Judges. If this is impracticable, Judges must indicate on the Test forms which parts they have judged. Not more than two parts shall be judged on the same day.

Part (a).—*A descent of not less than 2,500 feet, which should, if possible, be continuous without any intervening stretches of level or uphill. The course selected must provide ample opportunity for fast, straight* running, and must also include a fair proportion of steep and difficult ground.

Part (b).—A descent of not less than 1,000 feet on really difficult snow, such as hard, wind-swept, unbreakable crust, on which Lifted Stemming turns are practicable but Telemarks impossible, varied by breakable crust in which only Jump turns are practicable.

Part (c).—A descent of not less than 500 feet of difficult woodrunning in which continuous turns are just possible for a first-class runner.

The above represents a minimum, rather than a maximum. If Judges can devote sufficient time to the Test, each section may well be repeated on different days in order that the Judges may have ample opportunity of coming to a decision.

For a descent of about 500 feet, the candidate should lead in order to test his capacity for choosing a good line. During the rest of the Test one of the Judges must lead and must set a first-class speed. The other Judge must remain behind the candidate in order to compare his speed and steadiness with that of the leading Judge.

A First Class runner turns as little as possible and slows up as little as possible before each turn. His turns are done at a high speed on all but very steep ground.

The candidate must satisfy the Judges that his running combines high speed, thorough steadiness on difficult ground and difficult snow, and an easy, effortless control of his ski.

# SKIJUMPING TESTS.

GENERAL REGULATIONS.

1. The length of a jump shall be measured with a taut tape from the edge of the take-off to that point at which the hindermost ski touches the alighting track with the part immediately below the binding.

2. To constitute a standing jump the runner must not fall within a distance of 40 metres from the edge of the take-off or within a distance of 60 metres where the jump, as in the First Class Test, exceeds 30 metres. If the runner comes to a standstill without falling within this distance he will be held to have stood.

3. If a runner saves himself from falling by supporting himself with his hands, he shall be considered to have fallen.

# THIRD CLASS TEST (JUMPING).

1. Every Candidate is required to make two standing jumps of not less than 10 metres. Four attempts are allowed on the same day.

2. Any two Judges appointed by the Council for the Cross Country Skiing Tests are qualified to judge this Test.

## SECOND CLASS TEST (JUMPING).

1. Every Candidate is required to make two standing jumps of not less than 20 metres. Four attempts are allowed on any one day.

2. Any two Second Class Judges appointed by the Federal Council for Cross Country Skiing Tests may judge this Test. Any Candidate who has passed this Test may replace one of the Second Class Judges.

## FIRST CLASS TEST (JUMPING).

1. Every Candidate is required to make two standing jumps of not less than 30 metres. Four attempts are allowed on any one day.

2. Two Second Class Judges appointed by the Federal Council for Cross Country Skiing may judge this Test. Any Candidate who has passed the Second Class Jumping Test may act in place of one of the Second Class Judges.

2900257R00044

Printed in Great Britain
by Amazon.co.uk, Ltd.,
Marston Gate.